THE Gospel on the street

Paul's first letter to the Corinthians

IVAN T. BLAZEN

Pacific Press Publishing Association
Nampa, Idaho
Oshawa, Ontario, Canada

Edited by Kenneth R. Wade
Cover art by Lars Justinen
Designed by Michelle Petz

ISBN 0-8163-1411-X

97 98 99 00 01 • 5 4 3 2 1

Contents

Dedication

To my faithful secretary, Gayle Foster,
whose keen eyes, creative insights,
and dedicated effort were invaluable for this book.

Introduction

Private letters and public scrutiny

My mother taught me not to open other people's mail. I'll bet your mother did the same. Yet, here we are, ready to open Paul's personal letter to the church at Corinth. If you were the Corinthians, would you like the details of your private problems advertised to the whole world?

If your answer is no, why then do we read Paul's personal correspondence? You say, "Because it's Scripture." You are right, but that was not apparent at first. Do you think when Paul wrote 1 Corinthians he knew he was producing Scripture that would be joined to and in some ways surpass the Bible (the Old Testament) he revered as the Word of God? I doubt it.

However, while he may not have thought of himself as adding to the Scriptures, Paul was conscious of speaking God's word. To the Thessalonians he says: "We constantly give thanks to God for this, that when you received the word of God that you heard from us, you accepted it not as a human word but as what it really is, God's word, which is also at work in you believers" (1 Thess. 2:13).

So, when we read 1 Corinthians, we read it to hear God's message through the story of Paul's interaction with people who had real problems in their Christian faith and life. The Word of God always takes flesh, because that is where we can hear and understand it.

But remember, we are really not better than those we read

about. Thank God He was willing to speak to them so that He might also speak to us.

I invite you, then, to study 1 Corinthians with me. The most important thing you can do before you read each chapter of this book is to carefully read the Bible passage upon which it is based and pray for the illumination of the Holy Spirit to open your understanding and guide you into truth. *The* Book should come before this or any other book. Besides, what you read here will make the most sense if you have first become thoroughly familiar with what Scripture itself says. It will be very helpful if you will keep the Bible open for constant reference as you reflect on what is said here. I will use the New Revised Standard Version except where otherwise indicated.

A word about Corinth

What happens when the gospel comes into an urban center famous for its history, luxury, political and administrative power, commerce and trade, international tourism, athletics, diversity of races, nations, cultures, social standings, religions and philosophies, and pervasive licentiousness? How does Christianity fare in such an environment? Does it really take root, and will it be preserved in its essence or become tainted or transformed by the conditions in which it was born? Can one maintain an authentic Christian life in a pagan setting, a moral existence in an immoral context, and a gospel understanding in a sea of alien beliefs? First Corinthians gives us insight into early Christianity—how it relates to the world, and how believers relate to each other. The integrity of Christian identity and community are at stake. The issues which faced the urban Christians of Corinth are also valid for Christians today. First Corinthians supplies an apostolic corrective to the infiltration and interpretation of Christian faith and life by the "wisdom of this world," the mores of culture, and the morals of the masses.

Saints are imperfect people moving toward perfection. We are not growing to be saints, but saints growing to be like Christ!

Chapter 1

Acts 18:1-18; 1 Corinthians 1:1-9

MAKING SAINTS ISN'T EASY

Origins of mission in Corinth

It is a difficult task to be a missionary, evangelist, or pastor. Paul, who occupied all three of these callings, found that out, particularly in his dealings with his converts in Corinth.

Divine vision was the spark for Paul's unprecedented efforts to plant the gospel and grow the Church in Macedonia and Greece. During the night at Troas, Paul had a vision in which he heard a voice pleading with him to come and help Macedonia. He was convinced God was calling him to preach the gospel in that area (Acts 16:8-10). Soon there were colonies of believers in Philippi, Thessalonica, and Berea. His work in these places followed a pattern: proclamation led to conversion; then opposition forced withdrawal (16:11-17:15). The situation was not much better in Athens, where in response to his Areopagus sermon, some scoffed, others delayed consideration, and a few believed (17:16-32). No church was formed, and it seemed best to leave to seek more fertile ground in Corinth.

Here Paul was reviled in the synagogue when he tried to prove that Jesus was the Messiah, but Corinthians who heard him preach elsewhere believed and were baptized. Once again divine vision was the incentive for new mission. In the night the Lord revealed that Paul should not be afraid or silent, for many in the city were God's people. As a result, Paul labored for eighteen months in Corinth, publicizing the good news of Christ. Afterward, his Jewish opponents attempted to quash

7

his evangelistic work, but they failed, and Paul stayed in Corinth a considerable time longer. Despite opposition, divine power and human faithfulness had combined to found a significant church in this major crossroads of world travel (18:1-18).

Today the voice of God may still be heard, this time pleading with us: "Come and help throughout the earth, for there are yet many who are my people. Do not be afraid or silent." Once again, grasping the heavenly vision will inspire our gospel mission.

Communications with Corinth

While the founding of the Corinthian church must be looked upon as a triumph of the gospel and its messenger, Paul, a look at his interactions with the church shows that he had real difficulties with his new converts. From the information we have, we know that subsequent to his first visit, the long evangelistic stay in Corinth, Paul made another visit, projected a third, and wrote four letters to the church. Here's how it went:

1. After the founding of the community, but prior to 1 Corinthians, Paul wrote a letter admonishing the believers not to associate with immoral people in the church (1 Cor. 5:9-11).

2. Paul received news about difficulties in the church from the household of Chloe (1:11) and from a letter written by members of the congregation (7:1). This letter was probably carried by Stephanus, Fortunatus and Achaicus (16:17), who may have revealed even more of the situation.

3. In response to this information Paul wrote 1 Corinthians.

4. The problems must have continued, deepened, and become more personal, for Paul interrupted his work in Ephesus to make another visit to Corinth. We know of this second visit by way of inference from his statement that he intended to come to his converts a third time (2 Cor. 12:14; 13:1), and because he explicitly mentions a second visit (13:2). Though we do not have many details, this was a very painful visit for both Paul and his converts (2:1-3). He must have issued stern warnings about

Corinthian conduct but showed leniency as well (13:2).

5. Despite this painful visit the situation deteriorated, and Paul wrote another letter, filled with anguish and tears (2:4). This letter had a number of sides for, in addition to Paul's distress, its tone and content made the Corinthians grieve (7:8); it was a test of whether they would follow him in dealing with a moral problem in a forgiving way (2:5-10); and it contained an assurance of Paul's love for them (2:4).

6. Titus carried Paul's difficult letter to the Corinthian believers (2:13; 7:13), and Paul anxiously awaited his return with news of how they had received his message. However, his concern was so great that his patience grew thin, and he decided to find Titus on the route of his return (2:13; 7:5, 13). When they met, Paul was exhilarated by the joy of Titus, whose mind had been set at ease by the positive response of the church (7:13-16).

7. In consequence of this, Paul wrote 2 Corinthians, in which he expressed joy over reconciliation with his converts (chapters 1–7), gave directions concerning an important offering intended to create unity between Jewish and Gentile Christians (chapters 8, 9), and offered a spirited defense of his apostleship against a group of self-styled apostles from outside the church who were attacking his apostolic credentials and message and trying to undermine his relationship with the Corinthians (chapters 10-13).

A sanctified and spiritually gifted church

First Corinthians begins with a highly skilled introduction (1:1-9) in which Paul interweaves his positive acknowledgment of the status and gifts of the Corinthians with subtle signals of his concern for them. Though there were great tensions between him and his converts and significant problems in the life and thought of the church, in his introduction Paul affirms the church's connection with Christ and expresses gratitude for its enrichment by Christ. If one is going to deal with problem people, it is much better to begin with their good points. Highlighting the good supplies motivation for correcting what is defective. Paul's example teaches us to put the positive before the negative. A message of acceptance and care should precede any disapproval or criticism, and whatever tough things need to be said should not be to make anyone ashamed, but to admonish in a loving way (1 Cor. 4:14).

Paul writes not to the "church of Corinth," as if it were a separate entity, but to the "church of God *at* Corinth." The church is a universal reality with every local church being a part of this larger fellowship of believers. Despite differences due to geography, race, customs, or opinions, there is only "one faith, one baptism, one God and father of all" (Eph. 4:5, 6). This is why Paul strikes the note of unity when he speaks of "all those who in every place call on the name of our Lord Jesus Christ, both their Lord and ours" (1 Cor. 1:2). Since the Corinthians thought of themselves as a spiritually elite church, this was a most relevant comment. Individual churches and members are part of the larger whole.

By speaking of the "church *of God*," that is, the church that belongs to God, Paul uses a phrase unique to the Corinthian epistles which has implications for the sectarianism that existed in Corinth. Polarized groups in the church were expressing allegiance to various human leaders (1:10-12; 4:6).

It must have been disheartening for Paul to be the founder and pastoral father of a church which took more than a year and a half to establish (from A. D. 50-52) and then, within the space of three years (by A. D. 55), to see the erosion of the distinction between the gospel and the popular wisdom of the day, and the descent of his precious flock into major behavioral and theological problems.

Nevertheless, Paul designates his readers as "those who are sanctified in Christ Jesus, called to be saints." Paul is sincere in this, but it is a remarkable statement, given the shortcomings of the Corinthian Christians. The following list is quite stunning:

1. They were a factious, jealous, and quarrelsome group, dangerously close to destroying the church (1:11, 12; 3:3, 17).

2. They made great pretensions of wisdom, knowledge, and eloquence at the expense of the Cross as "foolishness" of preach-

ing (1:18-2:4; 3:18-20; 8:1, 2). Arrogance rather than humility characterized them (4:8-10, 18; 5:2).

3. Sexual immorality was tolerated and promoted in the church (5:1-13; 6:12-20).

4. Instead of seeking to resolve differences in a Christian way, believers were suing believers and even seeking to defraud them in pagan courts (6:1-8).

5. In contrast to the sexual libertines of 6:12-20, some promoted a dangerous sexual asceticism and even recommended divorce so that sex might be avoided (7:1-39).

6. Liberal disregard of weaker consciences and concentration upon personal rights evidenced a lack of love and responsibility toward others (chapters 8 and 9; 10:14-11:1).

7. A "once saved, always saved" theology was held, supported by a rather magical view of the Lord's Supper and baptism, which they saw as guarantees of salvation (10:1-13; 15:29).

8. Church worship was disturbed by violations of the contemporary dress code, disregard of the poor, drunkenness at the Lord's Supper, and such an unrestrained exercise of spiritual gifts that bedlam resulted and love for others was lost (11:2-14:40).

9. Some denied the basic Christian teaching of the future resurrection of the body (chapter 15).

In view of these strange practices and beliefs, how could Paul describe the Corinthians as already having been sanctified (the past tense used here stresses completed action with present results) and called to count themselves among God's saints (1:2)? How can sanctification be past if it is the work of a lifetime, and how can being a saint be a present reality if it is a future achievement?

Here we must note some very important points. To begin with, the words saint and sanctification represent one idea, not two, because they are built upon the same Greek root (*hagio*). The intimate relationship between these two words would have been much better conveyed if, in English, we had the word "*saint*ification" instead of "sanctification." Sanctification (or saintification) refers to God's setting people apart to belong to him, and "saints" is simply a designation of their new status. Next, sanctification, which makes one a saint, has two meanings in Scripture. In its primary sense it is a relational rather than a moral term. We did not belong to God but, because He set us apart, we now do. In this sense the word refers to that completed event in the past when God consecrated us to Himself. This is why 1 Corinthians 6:11 can say, using the past tense in Greek, that we already have been washed, sanctified, and justified. Furthermore, since the word sanctified is a relational term, it can even be placed before the word justified, another relational term referring to a right standing with God. Consequently, the order of the ideas "separated for God" and "rightly related to God" does not matter.

In another sense sanctification refers to the ethical process of lifelong growth in likeness to Christ that results from having been chosen to belong to Him. Paul argues from this very point. Those who have been set apart as God's people (saints), ought to act like it! Our moral life should square with the fact that God has made us His own. "For you were bought with a price; therefore glorify God in your body" (6:20).

So, imperfect though we are, we still are saints. And though we are saints, we must continually grow. We may have many defects of character and thought, as did the saints at Corinth, but we still belong to God, and, therefore, are called to constant improvement. Saints are imperfect people moving toward perfection. We are not growing to be saints, but saints growing to be like Christ! We have the inspiration and motivation to do this because we already belong to God, who daily gives us further opportunities to grow.

The appeal to become truly good persons is not that by doing so we can become saints, but rather that being saints already, we can become truly good people. Unfortunately, many of us have bought into the Catholic concept that saints are a very rare group of perfect people. In fact, according to this teaching, one is not a saint in this lifetime, but becomes one, often centuries later, by the action of the church. It is believed that since these saints lived as moral superstars and did so much more than is needed for salvation, their extra merits can be applied to run-of-the-mill people who are deficient in merit.

Not so in the New Testament! All of God's children, constituted as such by a relationship to Christ (notice "sanctified *in Christ Jesus*" [emphasis supplied] in 1:2), are saints. That is why Paul addresses almost every letter to the saints. Enfeebled and defective as we, God's saints, may be, we still are the objects of His supreme regard and love. And that love will one day have made us fully like itself.

I wish that conference official had known this the day I walked through the door at one end of an auditorium while he was entering at the other end. In a happy mood I enthusiastically called out: "Well, how are the saints?"

He looked at me with a scowl, and in slow, somber tones said: "There's no one here but sinners making their way into the kingdom of God!"

I knew I was in trouble and needed to make a comeback. So, as we drew nearer to each other, I said: "Well, if Paul could call the Corinthians saints, with all their faults, surely the august members of this conference must be saints!" My friend became angrier. Coming closer yet, I tried again: "As Adventists we don't hold the Catholic view that a saint is a perfect person who needs no improvement." He grew angrier still. Now we were face to face. This was it. I touched his arm and said: "The New Testament teaches that we become saints when we believe in Jesus. So, you are a saint whether you believe it or not!" I turned and walked away before his anger became unsaintly rage!

Gifts of grace

The grace Paul greets the Corinthians with (1:3) is the grace which has already been given them in Christ (1:4). As a result, the Corinthians have become spiritually enriched in Christ. Paul expresses thanks, for example, that they have been gifted with speech and knowledge of every kind (1:5), despite the fact that some have misused these gifts.

Paul will give a full list of gifts in 1 Corinthians 12, but in 1:6 he stresses what makes such spiritual giftedness possible. He says that Christians become enriched to the extent that the testimony of Christ's word in the gospel has found lodgment in their hearts (1:6). When the gospel is truly appropriated, we will not be lacking in *any* spiritual gift, says Paul, as we await the revelation of Christ at His second coming (1:7). The result of these gifts is that we will be strengthened until the end so that the blamelessness we have always wished for, and sometimes tried to reach for in our own strength, will be true of us when our Lord returns (1:8). The guarantee of this is not a power within us or because of our faithfulness (the self-confident Corinthians needed this reminder), but it is the guarantee of the faithfulness of God and the fellowship He has made possible with Jesus, His Son and our Lord. "God's faithfulness, Christ's fellowship" should be our spiritual motto.

When Paul speaks of the future coming of Jesus in his introduction, he is striking a note of great significance for the Corinthians who made so much of present enlightenment and transformation that some denied a future resurrection (15:12). Paul stresses that the fullness of salvation and revelation is yet to be at the coming of Christ (1:7). As he says elsewhere: "He who has begun a good work in you will bring it to completion at the day of Jesus Christ" (Phil. 1:6, RSV). Present Christian experience must always be oriented toward the future advent.

What this means is that we can make no claim to have arrived, as the Corinthians did, but our hope is in Christ and His arrival. That is the arrival that really matters. And when He comes, He will bring perfection with Him and end the imperfection of our understanding (1 Cor. 13:8-10). Our stance should be like Paul's: "Not that I have already obtained this or am already perfect; but I press on to make it my own, because Christ Jesus has made me his own.... One thing I do, forgetting what lies behind and straining forward to what lies ahead, I press on toward the goal for the prize of the upward call of God in Christ Jesus" (Phil. 3:12-14, RSV). For now our life is hidden with Christ, but when He appears, then we shall appear with Him in glory (Col. 3:3, 4). When Christ arrives, we will truly arrive!

For all of us who carry the banner of the crucified Christ,
special claims and divisive cliques must end.
In belonging to Jesus, we belong to each other.

Chapter 2

1 Corinthians 1:10-17; 3:1-23

UNSAINTLY SQUABBLES AND DANGEROUS SCHISMS

News about Corinth

"No news is good news"—how true that slogan is. Paul could have wished for no news rather than the report he received from members of the household of Chloe, who were knowledgeable about conditions in the Corinthian church. They informed him that there was strife in the church. So serious was the quarreling and factiousness that it threatened to move from heated debate into real schism in the Corinthian fellowship (1:10, 11). No wonder Paul emphasized the fellowship with Christ to which God had called them (1:9). If believers are one with Christ, they should be one with each other. Fellowship rather than feuds should characterize God's people. Paul makes a solemn appeal that they not let the situation get out of hand and allow rivalry to cause irreparable ruptures in the life of the church.

Sectarianism and superiority

What was all the contention about? Unbelievably, it concerned which group in the church had the upper hand as to leadership and wisdom! Some were claiming, "I belong to Paul," and others, "I belong to Apollos" or to "Cephas" or to "Christ." Four groups laying claim to superiority and expressing an inflated (literally "puffed up") attitude toward the others (4:6)! They did not realize that true love is never puffed up, arrogant, or conceited (13:4).

15

What can be said about these groups? Why were they formed? It was natural that some Corinthians would associate themselves with Paul for, after all, it was his eighteen months of labor that had founded the church. However, the fact that there were other groups and that Paul was unhappy about a group claiming his name (1:13-15) shows that his apostolic authority was in question with this church. His converts were clearly doing their own thing.

Apollos was a natural winner with others, for he possessed the trait Greeks loved most—the gift of rhetoric, which involved wisdom expressed with eloquence and aesthetic appeal. In a church where the gifts of speech and knowledge were prized (1:5), this orator from the famous city of Alexandria (Acts 18:24), with its philosophy, mysticism, and allegorical interpretations, must have made a real impression. In contrast, Paul seemed deficient in oratorical skills, lacked concern for worldly wisdom (1 Cor. 1:17; 2:1, 4; 2 Cor. 10:10), and was judged by the Athenians to be a "babbler," or literally, a "seed picker" (Acts 17:18.) This term refers to a person who gets a thought here and another there, but does not put them together into a deep and coherent philosophical system.

Some, perhaps Jewish Christians, may have looked to Cephas (Peter) as their leader since he had been with Jesus, was very prominent in the early church, and may have been thought to represent a more conservative position theologically, in contrast to Paul, whom some considered more revolutionary.

The Christ party may have represented a group which estimated itself in even more haughty terms than the others. While the other groups, if pressed, undoubtedly would have admitted that Christ was their ultimate spiritual head, this group claimed exclusive rights to Christ. Rather than speaking for every believer by saying "We *all* belong to Christ," members of this group spoke only of themselves as belonging to Him. The only proper answer to this assertion of unique privilege is to say with Paul: "If you are confident that you belong to Christ, remind yourself of this, that just as you belong to Christ, so also do we" (2 Cor. 10:7).

Belonging to the crucified Christ

In fact, that is just the point Paul wanted to get across to the Corinthians. Instead of members claiming to belong to various earthly leaders, the entire congregation should think of itself as belonging only to Christ. Against factiousness and rivalry the question must be raised: "Has Christ been divided?" (1 Cor. 1:13). If Christ cannot be chopped up into pieces and each group given a separate share, how can His body, the church, be divided? This is absurd, and completely out of harmony with the fact that "we were all baptized into one body" (12:13).

To emphasize his point Paul asked another important question, which could have been asked about any earthly leader: "Was Paul crucified for you? Or were you baptized in the name of Paul?" (1:13). The answer could only be "No!" Jesus alone was crucified for them, and only into His name was anyone baptized. For all of us who carry the banner of the crucified Christ, special claims and divisive cliques must end. In belonging to Jesus, we belong to each other.

Spiritual immaturity and fleshly inclination

For Paul, the existence of cliques, with the jealousy and quarreling they engender, show that the church members involved are not spiritual grownups, but fleshly infants with purely human inclinations (3:1-4). This evaluation must have been a blow to Corinthian elitism and egocentricity. They probably were as shocked and affronted as we would be if the same charge was leveled at us as a result of our pride and bickering.

But Paul's evaluation gets tougher yet. He says that we cannot help being *made of flesh*, which is the meaning of the word used in 3:1 (the KJV says "carnal"), but we are not to be *characterized by the flesh*, which is the meaning of the word occurring twice in 3:3. To be made of flesh is not negative by itself, for we were created flesh. However, since we are related to the eternal God, we are not to be only flesh, but persons led by the Spirit of God. When flesh stands in opposition to Spirit, as it does in 3:1, it becomes negative. It refers to natural man, one who does not follow the direction of the Spirit, as opposed to spiritual man, who does. When Paul says in 3:1 that he could not address the Corinthians as spiritual people, he implies that they considered themselves to be spiritual. But actions speak louder than words, and Paul was now judging their actions, something unnecessary for truly spiritual people (2:15). People of the Spirit would not be filled with jealousy and strife (3:3). These are attributes of the flesh, and they stand in contrast to the fruit of the Spirit which is "love, joy, peace, patience, kindness, generosity, faithfulness, gentleness, and self control." In fact, "those who belong to Christ Jesus have crucified the flesh" and therefore are not to be "conceited, competing against one another, envying one another" (Gal 5:19-26). How do we in today's church measure up to this description?

Paul's most frequent use of the word "flesh" does not refer to our material composition, but to living in a spiritually and morally self-centered, self-indulgent, and hurtful way. As God's imperfect saints, we must constantly ask whether our disposition, deliberations, and demeanor represent flesh or Spirit. According to Scripture, these two principles war against each other for the mastery of Christians. Flesh would return us to bondage and death, but the Spirit would give us freedom over the flesh and eternal life (Rom. 8:5-9, 12, 13; 13:14; Gal 5:13, 16, 17, 24, 25; 6:7, 8).

Can there be such a thing as a "carnal Christian"? Perhaps, if this means that one may sometimes act on the fleshly level due to lack of knowledge of the full moral implications of the gospel—as is often true of recent converts like the Corinthians— or temporary lapses from Christian principles because of immaturity or weakness. However, if what is meant by "carnal Christian" is one who *persists* in characteristics of the flesh as a *lifestyle*, then the answer must be No, for Scripture declares that those who make it a practice to do such things will not inherit God's kingdom (Gal. 5:21; 1 Cor. 6:9, 10). It has been rightly said that "the character is revealed, not by occasional good deeds and occasional misdeeds, but by the tendency of the habitual words and acts" (*Steps to Christ*, 57, 58).

Co-workers with God

Because of their predilection to exalt humans and fight for precedence by attaching themselves to certain leaders, the

Corinthians needed to understand the correct function of leaders. Paul addresses the issue by declaring that he and Apollos, persons associated with the two leading Corinthian factions, were only servants through whom the Corinthians came to believe. Paul first came as a missionary (Acts 18:1-11) and, when he left, Apollos took up his mission (18:24-28). The two missions were interrelated, for Paul planted (did the initial work), and Apollos watered (did the follow-up work, 1 Cor. 3:6). They were not heroes, but servants and coworkers in God's service (3:8, 9). Why then should they be given an elevated status, particularly over opposing rather than collaborating groups? Exaltation belongs only to God, for He alone makes the growth of the seed possible (3:6, 7).

Humility and equality

In what Paul says here about himself and Apollos, we see real humility toward God and equality toward each other. In the church of God there can be no spiritual hierarchy, for every believer is on a par in Christ and possesses all things in Christ, including leaders (3:21-23). The master is not greater than the servant (see Philemon 16, 17). Peter beautifully expresses the attitude leaders need: "Now as an elder myself . . . I exhort the elders among you to tend the flock of God. . . . Do not lord it over those in your charge, but be examples to the flock. And when the *chief shepherd* appears, you will win the crown of glory. . . . And all of you must clothe yourselves with humility in your dealings with one another, for 'God opposes the proud, but gives grace to the humble.' Humble yourselves therefore under the mighty hand of God, so that he may exalt you in due time" (1 Pet. 5:1-6, emphasis supplied).

Building or destroying God's temple

Paul's imagery shifts quickly. Thinking in agricultural images, with himself as the planter and Apollos as the waterer, he describes the church as God's field (1 Cor. 3:9). Then, turning to architectural figures, he depicts the Corinthian church as God's building. In constructing an edifice, the foundation is of first importance, because nothing meant to last can be built without a solid foundation. Here Paul declares that he was the one who laid the foundation for the Corinthian church. He calls himself "a wise architect," which is the literal rendering of his words. However, the Greek word, *architekon*, which he uses, does not refer to the designer of the building, as it does today, but to the one who engineers the building project. In coupling "architect" with the word "wise" Paul is claiming that he is a "master builder," an expert. The use of "wise" was especially pertinent to the Corinthian situation where members were claiming that their superior wisdom was manifested in their choice of leaders. On the contrary, Paul says that true wisdom was manifested when he laid the only true foundation of the church, Jesus Christ (3:11). That is *the* name and *the* foundation. Those who build on that foundation must keep their thoughts oriented toward Christ, not to human leaders. How could one build on Jesus and say "I belong to Paul" or "to Apollos"? It just doesn't make sense.

Paul's primary concern is about how the Corinthians will build upon the foundation of Jesus. The vocation of those who come after him is to solidify the church. To accomplish this, the quality of the materials they use needs to match the superior quality of the foundation, especially since they are building a temple. Two categories of materials are described: gold, silver, and precious stones; and wood, hay, and stubble. These materials, arranged in descending order, contrast the precious with the common, and what would be appropriate for a temple, where God's presence will be manifested, with what is used in an average home. More importantly, Paul is differentiating what would be more durable and resistant to fire with what would burn quickly. This fits the idea of the day of testing by fire in verse 13. Paul admonishes that each builder must make careful choices, because of the nature of the building and the fire inspection it must undergo (verse 10). It really matters how one builds. If the builder wants anything to show for his work, he must put good quality and skill into it.

Paul's metaphorical language has to do with the building up of the church of God. The kinds of issues involved are represented in a series of questions. Is the church being built up in unity, mutual love and respect, edification and care? Are church members working together and the corporate nature of the church being fostered? Are members being visited and their problems addressed? Are necessary funds being expended for worship, instruction, evangelism, and discipling? Are lines of communication being forged between diverse groups in the church, such as young and old, women and men, black and white? Are members involved in helping the widows, orphans, poor, divorced, suffering, and minorities? Are the saints being equipped for service?

The work of each builder will become visible, for the "Day" (of the Lord) will disclose it. The fire of the judgment will test the building project and burn up whatever was poorly done (1 Cor. 3:13; compare Joel 2:3; Mal. 4:1; 2 Thess. 1:7, 8). Paul says that "if what has been built on the foundation survives, the builder will receive a reward" (1 Cor. 3:14), a "commendation from God" (4:5).

It would be an extreme deprivation to miss God's commendation. With this thought in mind, Paul continues: "If the work is burned up, the builder will suffer loss; the builder will be saved, but only as through fire" (3:15). Some people have taken false security from this verse, thinking it means that no matter how shoddy our work, we can relax; we will be saved anyway. "Once saved always saved, no matter what!" This is not what Paul means! In verse 15 he is not really giving an assurance. The words "saved, but only as through fire" must be interpreted correctly. Catholicism has used them to support its doctrine of purgatory, a place in the afterlife which purges from sin in preparation for entry into heaven. This view interprets "through fire" as "by means of fire." However, the word "through," while sometimes indicating means, here signifies movement through a location, as in, "I walked through the house." What Paul pictures is a building which begins to burn while the builder is in it. The building has been made of an inferior material (wood, hay or stubble) which is very flammable and burns quickly. As the flaming embers are crashing down, the builder can only escape by running "through the fire" to get outside before it is too late. The picture is that of a person barely making it, getting to safety only "by the skin of his teeth," certainly not one of security and safety regardless of what one has done. Implicit is a warning to be careful!

If those who have built poorly scarcely make it out alive, what will happen to those who try to destroy God's church (3:16, 17)? They will not make it at all! No possibility of salvation exists for them as for the poor builder. In this scenario the church is specifically called God's temple (the term comes from a Greek word which means "to dwell"). All believers form this temple, and it is holy because God's Spirit dwells in it. No one can try to destroy it with impunity. This would be to sin against the Spirit—in a real sense, the unforgivable sin. Let all ancient and modern destroyers beware! God will be a consuming fire to all who would consume his people (Heb. 10:26, 27, 31; 12:29).

True wisdom

First Corinthians 3 closes with two major thoughts. First, there is an admonition to avoid deception about wisdom (1 Cor. 3:18-20). Much better to have the wisdom of so-called fools—those who believe the gospel—than to be wise in "this age" (standing for "the present evil age," as in Gal. 1:4). The wisdom of this age is foolishness with God. Next, Paul specifies what he means by truly becoming wise. It is to avoid boasting of attachment to human leaders since they actually belong to the members of the church (3:21). Leadership does not dominate the church, but serves it. Indeed, everything, whether present or future, belongs to believers, and they belong to Christ, who belongs to God (3:22, 23). The wonderful paradox is that by belonging to Christ, all the riches of God come to belong to us. Let us boast in God, not in man!

*Examine any philosophy, no matter how highly sophisticated,
and you will not find a loving, redeeming God. . . .
The conception of God and His salvation, as revealed in the
story of Christ and the cross, is totally unique.*

Chapter 3

1 Corinthians 1:17–2:16

GOD'S FOOLISHNESS VERSUS HUMAN WISDOM

The center of the gospel

What would you do if you were the pastor of a faction-ridden congregation? How would you try to get your people to give up their pride, arrogance, judgmentalism, and contentiousness and be united with one another in humility, mutual respect, and cooperation? Here is what a pastor friend of mine did when his congregation split into rival (and sometimes hostile!) factions over the issue of where their new church building should be located. He decided to center *all* of his preaching, each and every week, on Jesus and nothing but Jesus—His story, His mission, His message. He did this for about three years until the hearts of his people melted under the loving influence of Jesus, the great Master Builder. Sure, there were a few who still insisted on their own way, which is not love's way (1 Cor. 13:5), but most of the people came together in heart and mind and built the new church.

What would happen if we seriously lived the inspired advice we have been given and spent a thoughtful hour *each day* contemplating the life of Jesus (*Desire of Ages*, 83)? An unbelievable unity might emerge in the church, and, filled with divine incentive, we might really build a holy temple to the Lord on the solid foundation of Jesus.

Paul took this tack with the Corinthians. He told them that he had been sent to proclaim the gospel in such a way that *its* power rather than his rhetorical skill would be manifested

(1:17). And what was the center of this gospel? The message of the crucified Christ. That such a message could be true, or the source of unity, seemed so unbelievable that some called it foolishness, in effect rejecting it. Their denial placed them among the perishing. But to those who chose to be part of God's saving activity, the Cross was experienced as the power of God (1:18). As 2 Corinthians 2:15, 16 shows, the same gospel can have two responses and two effects: belief results in life; unbelief in death.

Have you noticed the contrast between foolishness and power in verse 18? This seems strange indeed, for we would expect Paul to contrast foolishness with wisdom. But here he does not speak of the Cross as wisdom, for he wants to make the point that the Cross is not about an intellectual idea or speculative system of thought. We are not saved by what we think—though thinking and theology do play an important role in understanding the meaning of salvation. We are saved *by what God does!* The good news of the gospel is about God's powerful intervention in human history to rescue the lost from sin, Satan, suffering, and death. This is not merely an idea, but an event which demands our experiential appropriation, not merely our mental assent.

According to Romans 1:16, 17, Paul is not ashamed of the gospel (as are those mentioned in 1 Cor. 1:23-26) precisely because it is the power of God which leads to salvation. Divine power is a theme in 1 Corinthians (1:17, 18, 24; 2:4, 5). The gospel message has to do with God's power, and it takes just this power for humans to be saved. Without it we cannot move from sin to righteousness, guilt to freedom, fear to faith, hate to love, or death to life.

Bring on the wise men

Paul was not beyond using satire to reproach those who thought so highly of human wisdom and its teachers! He quotes Isaiah 29:14, where God says He will destroy the wisdom of the wise and thwart the discernment of the discerning. Paul uses this text, which originally spoke of God bypassing human wisdom in saving Israel from the Assyrians, and turns it against the Corinthian obsession with wisdom teachers (1 Cor. 1:19).

Paul says in effect: Bring on your wise, your scribes, and your debaters. Let's have a look at them! Has God not shown their worldly wisdom to be foolishness? (1:20). The idea of the wise man probably has its background in that group of rhetorically refined wisdom teachers who traveled from place to place winning converts by tickling the intellectual fancies of the people and presenting their philosophical views with highly ornamental oratory. These traveling salesmen for wisdom were known as Sophists (based on the Greek word *sophia*, meaning wisdom), from which we get the English word sophistry, referring to clever and subtle but sometimes misleading reasoning. The "wise" may well be the lead category, with "scribe" and "debater" as subcategories. Greek teachers were not called scribes, but Jewish theologians, lawyers, and rabbis were; so here we have the Jewish wise man. The Greek or Gentile wise man is called the "debater." By the use of both Jewish and Gentile categories, Paul prepares the way for his discussion of Jews and Greeks in 1:22-24.

How did God make the wisdom of this world foolish? The rest of the chapter gives us the answer. Paul first states that a special way of knowing God was needed because, when the landscape of human thought is surveyed, it is plain that the world did not come to know God through its wisdom (1:21). Romans 1:18-32 paints a picture of where human reason inventing religion leads: from idolatry straight to immorality. But further, examine any philosophy, no matter how highly sophisticated, and you will not find a loving, redeeming God, as is the Father of our Lord Jesus Christ. The conception of God and His salvation, as revealed in the story of Christ and the Cross, is totally unique. Not only that, but from a worldly-wise point of view, it is downright foolish! Salvation by believing in a crucified Messiah? Ridiculous! (1 Cor. 1:21, 23).

Among the two major classes of people at this time in history, the Jews were seeking for miraculous signs, while the Greeks (Gentiles) hankered for rhetorically packaged wisdom (1:22). Miraculous verification and speculative subtlety were what they desired. Instead, they were offered Christ crucified! Whoever heard of such a thing? According to 2:9, 10, no one.

Human logic and insight could never have led to this under-standing of the means of salvation.

The Cross as scandal

The idea that this was God's way of leading us to glory (2:7) was a "stumbling block to Jews" (1:23). Why? In considering this it should be noted that "stumbling block," something that trips a person up, may not be the best way to translate the word Paul uses. The Greek word is *skandalon*, from which we derive the English word "scandal," meaning something shame-ful or disgraceful. The cross totally horrified and scandalized the Jews. It was an implement of torture reserved by Rome for unruly slaves, criminals, or revolutionaries. The sufferer, flogged until his flesh was torn away from his body, often ex-posing his internal organs, was stripped naked and spiked to a wooden beam and cross bars, hung before the gaze of the curi-ous and scoffers. The crucified person, barely able to breathe, with gravity pulling his body downward, was left to suffer the most excruciating torments. The hymn has it right: "On a hill far away stood an old rugged cross, the emblem of suffering and shame." To speak of "Christ crucified" was an impossible combination of words issuing in an absolutely unimaginable thought. In those days the major concept of the Messiah was that of a warrior king, like David, who would defeat the en-emies of God's people. To see Him put to death by those very enemies was to be forced to the devastating conclusion of the two Emmaus travelers: Jesus was not the one to redeem Israel (Luke 24:21). Deuteronomy 21:23 states that "anyone hung on a tree is under God's curse." Thus, for the Jews, Jesus' crucifix-ion could only mean that He stood not merely under the judg-ment of Rome, but worse, under the wrath of God! If faith could only have seen:

> It's true, dear friends, it's true
> Christ suffered the curse
> Upon the cruel tree
> But he hung there for you,
> He suffered there for me.

For first-century Jews "Christ crucified" was a blasphemous contradiction of terms, for "Christ" meant divine victory, and "crucified" meant human defeat. If Jesus was victim rather than victor, He could not be the Messiah. Furthermore, Rome was an idolatrous nation. Could idolaters conquer God's true deliverer? Jews felt wholly justified in their rejection of Jesus because He did not bring the restoration of Israel or universal peace, justice, and knowledge of God, as the Old Testament prophets had predicted of the coming kingdom (Isa. 2:2-4; 9:1-7; 11:1-9). If He did not inaugurate the expected Messianic Age, how could He possibly be the Messiah?

In any case, the scandal of the Cross was deep in Jewish minds. Neither the sacrificial system nor Isaiah 53 were interpreted by Jews as references to a suffering Messiah because such a concept would have conflicted with their concept of the Messiah as a conquering king. God's servant in Isaiah 52:13–53:12 was thought to refer to Israel, for this identification is made elsewhere in Isaiah (Isa. 41:8, 9; 42:19; 44:1, 2, 21; 45:4; 48:20; 49:3, 5, 6). Thus, it was thought that Israel suffered not merely for her own sins, but also for the sins of the nations who afflicted her.

The Cross as foolishness

While the Jews found the Cross totally scandalous, the Gentiles found the message of salvation through Jesus' crucifixion absolutely absurd (1 Cor. 1:23). In a drawing discovered in the ruins of Rome, a slave is pictured as falling down before a crucified figure with the head of a donkey. Beneath are the words: "Alexamenos worships his god." To Christians across the centuries who have hallowed the crucifixion, this is blasphemy, but among first-century Gentiles the blasphemy was that anyone would worship at the shrine of one who had been crucified.

Paul's proclamation that God was reconciling the world to Himself in the crucifixion of Christ (2 Cor. 5:19) was viewed as totally discordant with wisdom. After all, God was spirit; how could He involve Himself with flesh and death? God was known as the "unmoved Mover" (Aristotle's view); so how could He be moved by the specter of human sin and woe? If anything moved

Him He would no longer be the First Cause.

The God of the Greeks was characterized by *apatheia*, the Greek word from which we get the word "apathy," meaning "indifference." Among the Greeks the word had the deeper meaning of "not able to feel." To them God was incapable of *pathos* or seeing a situation as *pathetic*, over which he could then become *sympathetic* or *empathetic*. Indeed, as God, He was necessarily indifferent to human affairs.

They believed that human reason reaches up to grasp the reality of this unfeeling God, but God does not reach down to save sinful, suffering human beings. To them, just as Christian thought failed to reach the heights of enlightenment but descended to the depths of absurdity, so the Christian message was expressed, not in the highs of rhetorical discourse, but in the lows of uncultured speech. They also frowned upon what Paul took pride in: that not many wise, powerful, or noble were chosen by God (1 Cor. 1:26).

Paul accepted the charge against the lowly Cross, and the lowly classes to which it appealed, by declaring that since man's greatest wisdom and speech had not discovered or described the true God, God chose what was seemingly foolish and weak to shame the wise and strong (1:27, 28). His purpose was that no one might boast before Him since He alone, not human reason, ability, might, or accomplishment, is the source of our life (1:29, 30). This life is centered in Christ Jesus who is God's true wisdom. He, not philosophy or rhetoric, effects our righteousness (right standing with Him), sanctification (belonging to Him and growing to His likeness), and redemption (liberation from evil now and at the end of time). Therefore, all Corinthian boasting in their heroes, themselves, and their gifts should shift entirely to their Lord (1:30, 31).

The reason Paul did not proclaim the gospel to the Corinthians "in lofty words or wisdom" (2:1) was because he wanted the focus to be completely on God and His saving activity. Though lacking formal training in rhetoric (2 Cor. 11:6) and judged by trained orators as having contemptible speech (2 Cor. 10:10), Paul knew how to display beautiful forms of rhetoric (1 Cor. 4:8-13; 13:1-13; 2 Cor. 4:8-12). However, "he had purposely presented the gospel in its simplicity" (*The Acts of the Apostles*, 270) because he wanted the evidence of God's Spirit and power to be present so that the faith of his converts "might rest not on human wisdom but on the power of God" (1 Cor. 2:5).

In the same vein Paul later describes the treasure of the gospel as being housed in earthen pots (lowly humans like himself) so that the transcendent power might be shown to belong to God and not His earthly witnesses (2 Cor. 4:7). It was Paul's view that ministers are not to proclaim themselves, but Jesus Christ as Lord and themselves as His servants (4:5).

Those who preach and teach today need to have the same dependence upon God, emphasis on His power, and focus on Christ as did Paul. It is not only the Corinthians who could fall into the trap of thinking that eloquent wisdom will bring greatness.

For all his stress on the "foolishness" of the gospel so as to counter Corinthian claims, Paul teaches that for mature believers, the gospel as presented in its simplicity really is wisdom. This wisdom is not that of human reason, however, but of divine revelation, which discloses God's mystery (1 Cor. 2:6, 7). For Paul, a mystery is something that previously was hidden, but now is made known (Rom. 16:25, 26). Paradoxically put, it is God's open secret. Paul says this mystery was decreed before the ages, meaning in eternity past (2:7). Thus, the revelation of its content can only be a gift from God, not man's attainment. It is God's plan to deliver us from human folly and lead us all the way to glorification in the future. The futurity of glory was something the Corinthians needed to understand, for, as will become apparent, they believed their glorification had already become reality.

First Corinthians 2:9, with its reference to what humans have not seen, heard, or conceived, is sometimes understood incorrectly as a reference to our inability to know anything about what heaven is like. However, this is not the real subject here. In the context, it refers not to the glorified state itself, but to the means by which glorification is reached. There is only one means, the cross of Christ (2:2). This is what no human faculty has ever perceived (2:9).

In 2:8 Paul says that if the rulers of this age had understood that God was working salvation and ultimate glorification through the Cross, they would not have crucified the Lord of glory. Their plan to destroy Christ was the very means used by God to bring salvation! Not much wisdom or spiritual vision on their part! But what was not known has now been revealed to believers through God's Spirit "so that we may understand the gifts bestowed on us by God" (2:10, 12). To deny that God's saving benefits come through the Cross would be to have the spirit of the world—the very thing some Corinthians were in danger of—rather than the Spirit of God, which truly spiritual persons possess and which brings spiritual discernment (2:13, 14).

What does this have to do with the Corinthians? Everything! Paul is leading them to reflect on whether they, with all their claims to wisdom, are really spiritual after all. True, believers do "have the mind of Christ" (2:16), but this only deepens the question about Corinthian spirituality. In important ways they did not reflect Christ's mind, and thus Paul could not speak to them as "spiritual people, but rather as people of the flesh, as infants in Christ" (3:1). Putting it charitably, they had not grown to spiritual maturity. They still needed milk (3:2).

This chapter is a call to all Christians to make Christ crucified the center of all theology and experience. The witness of the church to the world cannot succeed if we, the church's members, emphasize our own wisdom, status, ability, and superiority to others. However, if we focus on Christ and His Cross, forgetting ourselves, the uplifted Christ will draw all people to Himself.

The practical significance of the Cross and the results of witnessing to it have not been better presented than in the following extended quotation from God's messenger:

> The consecrated messengers who in the early days of Christianity carried to a perishing world the glad tidings of salvation, allowed no thought of self-exaltation to mar their presentation of Christ and Him crucified. They coveted neither authority nor

preeminence. Hiding self in the Saviour, they exalted the great plan of salvation, and the life of Christ, the Author and Finisher of this plan. . . .

If those who today are teaching the Word of God, would uplift the cross of Christ higher and still higher, their ministry would be far more successful. If sinners can be led to give one earnest look at the cross, if they can obtain a full view of the crucified Saviour, they will realize the depth of God's compassion and the sinfulness of sin.

Christ's death proves God's great love for man. It is our pledge of salvation. To remove the cross from the Christian would be like blotting the sun from the sky. . . .

Through the cross we learn that the heavenly Father loves us with a love that is infinite. Can we wonder that Paul exclaimed, "God forbid that I should glory, save in the cross of our Lord Jesus Christ"? Galatians 6:14. It is our privilege also to glory in the cross, our privilege to give ourselves wholly to Him who gave Himself for us. Then, with the light that streams from Calvary shining in our faces, we may go forth to reveal this light to those in darkness (*The Acts of the Apostles*, 209, 210).

We are not called by God to success or popularity,
but to a ministry of faithfulness.

Chapter 4

1 Corinthians 4

PRIVILEGE AND POWER VERSUS RIFFRAFF AND RUBBISH

The fourth chapter of Corinthians is the high point of what Paul has been saying so far. Here we learn what Christian life and service is all about.

Trustworthy servants and stewards

In verses 1-5 Paul returns to the issue first raised in 3:5-9: the true position and role of himself and Apollos. "Think of us in this way. . . ." he says. The Corinthians had pegged them as party leaders and celebrities, but Paul claims they are "servants of Christ and stewards of God's mysteries" (4:1). The Greek word for servant here (*hyperetes*) is different from the word used in 3:5 (*diakonos*, from which we get "deacon"). Both words can be translated "servant," but *hyperetes*, as Luke 1:2 and Acts 26:16 show, meant something like an "official witness" and was used as such in Roman courts and civil administration. In other words, the job of Paul and Apollos was to testify to the word of God. Further, they were stewards, a term used for a slave who, in his master's absence, had charge of his household and its affairs. Both words have a double emphasis. They stress that the apostles are *under* authority to Christ and God, but *in* authority over the people of God. Being under authority, their trademark must be trustworthiness and faithfulness (4:2). Any authority they possess is exclusively in the context of God's will and service.

Therefore, those who are church leaders today have no authority in and of themselves. When the connection with God's will is broken, that authority is lost. Thus, the big word is accountability, as Jesus' parable of the dishonest steward shows (Luke 16:1, 2). We are not called by God to success or popularity, but to a ministry of faithfulness. No matter what church office we hold, with whatever prestige it has, we are to constantly recognize that we are still servants, strictly accountable to do the Lord's bidding. We need to remember that we will one day face God as our judge (1 Cor. 4:4, 5).

According to 4:2, God's stewards are in charge of His mysteries, the formerly hidden but now disclosed purposes of God. They are to testify to the revealed truth of the gospel which centers in Christ crucified. When they faithfully carry out this commission, as Paul did, it is irrelevant whether they are judged as to the quality of their eloquence or wisdom by people like the self-inflated Corinthians or, for that matter, by any human court (4:3). Actually, the word used in 4:3 is not "court" but "day." Paul is unconcerned about any human day in court. He uses the word day here in contrast to the Day (of the Lord) in 3:13. That Day will test every person's work; so it is presumptuous and premature for humans to pronounce judgment in their little day. God alone is capable of judging what humans cannot see, the deeds done in secret and the hidden purposes of the heart (4:5). As far as Paul's self-evaluation is concerned, he says that he is not conscious of anything against himself. He is not talking generally here, as if to claim that he has no shortcomings in his life. Rather, as God's steward, he is not aware of having failed his duty or done any wrong to the Corinthians. He is not overconfident, however, for he knows that there is a judgment that transcends his own—the judgment of the Lord (4:4).

There is real spiritual health in what Paul says here. Two truths are held in proper tension: he has an inner sense of peace, yet feels answerable to God. As we live our lives and do the Lord's work, both of these elements should characterize us. Peace is necessary to carry on our work for God, and accountability is necessary to keep peace from forgetting God's high standard. As Paul says in 1 Corinthians 15:10, God's grace to him, with the peace it brings, was not in vain. On the contrary, he worked harder than anyone.

Paul's healthy-mindedness is also shown in the last statement of verse 5. He says that workers will receive commendation when the judgment takes place at the coming of the Lord. He expects the outcome of his case, as well as that of other workers, to be good. Though he feels accountable, he is not fretful, but assured. Everyone who has placed his faith in Christ and has done his work should not be fearful of the outcome. Paul expects commendation rather than condemnation (probably a hint that his critics should try the same!) What Paul says here about his work holds true for the larger question of the ultimate salvation of believers. When we have given our lives to Christ, we should not fear His judgment. As 1 Thessalonians 5:9, 10 says: "God has destined us not for wrath but for obtaining salvation through our Lord Jesus Christ, who died for us."

Proper discrimination

One further word about judging. Paul does not feel that his Corinthian converts should judge him. Did he mean the church should make no judgments whatever? No! In chapter 5, for example, he instructs the church to execute judgment upon an immoral member. In verses 12-13 he explicitly says that the church, while not able to judge outsiders, should judge people within its midst whose moral life is contrary to the gospel. Is Paul a hypocrite, saying one thing in one place and something else in another? Not at all! He does something similar to what Jesus did in the Sermon on the Mount. There Jesus said: "Judge not, that you be not judged" (Matt. 7:1, RSV), and yet later said: "Do not give what is holy to dogs; and do not throw your pearls before swine" (Matt. 7:6). The latter text clearly calls for discrimination and evaluation. However, it is one thing to discriminate between the good and the bad, and another to blatantly and uncompassionately condemn, looking only for the bad. For the Corinthians to give Paul poor marks when he had worked so hard for them did not comport with gospel truth or Christian character.

Exalting the Word and humbling the self

Paul wanted the Corinthians to know that although he was speaking about himself and Apollos, it was for their benefit, not his own. By describing Apollos and himself as servants and stewards whose accountability would be appraised in the judgment, he wanted them to learn to be accountable as well. Since they were God's people, the written Word was to be their guide. They were not to go contrary to its principles by being "puffed up in favor of one against another" (1 Cor. 4:6). Underlying their self-inflation and discrimination against others was a misconception of Christian existence, as 4:8-13 shows. It is remarkable that of the seven New Testament occurrences of the word translated "puffed up," six of them occur in 1 Corinthians (4:6, 18, 19; 5:2; 8:1; 13:4). No wonder Paul, in his great chapter on love, contends that "love vaunteth not itself, is not puffed up" (13:4, KJV). Self-exaltation and putting others down does not breathe of God's Spirit. A fleshly walk comes from a fleshly mind, but Christians are to have the mind of Christ (2:15), which expresses itself in self-sacrificing, humble love and service to others (Phil. 2:2-8). In God's eyes the one who exalts himself shall be humbled, but he who humbles himself shall be exalted in the day of God's judgment (Matt. 23:12; Luke 14:11; 18:14). Jesus is the great exemplar of this exaltation by God (Phil. 2:9-11). The question for each of us is whether we are going to follow Him or our own inclinations.

Why should anyone engage in self-exaltation in the first place? When we realize that every spiritual endowment is a gift from God, why would any of us boast of superiority to others (1 Cor. 4:7)? Why be conceited over something which is strictly a matter of God's grace? Indeed, as Paul said earlier, if anyone is going to boast, let it be in the Lord (1:31).

There really are only two things to do with a gift from God: Thank Him for it, and use it to help others. Instead, the Corinthians were thumbing their own suspenders! We modern Christians would never do that, would we?

The difference beliefs can make

From light sarcasm in 4:7 Paul moves to heavy irony in 4:8-13 to get his point across. What true Christianity is about is at stake in this section. The Corinthians thought it was about reigning with Christ—*now*! They saw themselves as rich and regal, spiritual millionaires. For them the kingdom had already come, and they were seated at its tables, enjoying the banquet and luxuriating in the rich splendor of it all. They had arrived! Here we have the Laodicean condition before John's message to Laodicea was even given.

What is going on here? It has to do with eschatology, the study of last things. The Corinthians held a realized eschatology, meaning they believed God's salvation had been completed for them. Nothing more was needed other than the shedding of this earthly body. Most Christians throughout the ages, however, have believed in a future eschatology. Much still needs to happen, for while we have been forgiven and are in the process of sanctification, we are not all the way home. Cancer and countless other diseases need to be conquered; hatred and violence need to cease; evil, suffering, and death must end; and resurrection and exaltation must take place. In a realized eschatology, God's final salvation is thought to be already experienced in the enlightenment and transformation of the self and the realization of our true identity as spiritual beings rather than physical. No need to worry further, then, about sin's inroads. It cannot penetrate to the new self.

Sounds like New Age doctrine, doesn't it? As strange as it may seem to us today, the Corinthians held a view like that found in 2 Timothy 2:18, where the claim was made that "the resurrection has already taken place." Paul names those who held this teaching and says that wickedness rather than righteousness was the effect of it (2 Tim. 2:16-19).

The Corinthians had this very problem. Because some had replaced the teaching of the future resurrection of the body with the idea that their resurrection or transformation had already occurred, they believed that all things had become lawful to them. As a result, moral anarchy set in. A man was having sex with his stepmother (1 Cor. 5:1); Christians were defrauding each other in heathen courts (6:7, 8), and church members were visiting prostitutes (6:15, 16). Unbelievably, these things were not considered immoral but signs of Corinthian freedom from any further corrupting influences of the flesh! They could act as libertines (6:12-21) or ascetics (7:1-6) because the flesh did not matter any more. That is why Paul says in his resurrection chapter: "Do not be deceived: 'Bad company [with those who deny the future resurrection] ruins good morals.' Come to a sober and right mind, and sin no more; for some people have no knowledge of God" (15:33, 34).

In contrast to the Corinthians, who felt they had already received their heavenly inheritance and had begun to reign with Christ, Paul taught that the resurrection and end of time was still future (15:24); that only Christ is reigning now, and putting down God's enemies (15:25, 26); and that the real and wonderful gifts we have received in the present are only a down payment or guarantee of what will be (2 Cor. 1:22). Until then, "we walk by faith, not by sight" (5:7).

Bearing the Cross

Paul says, in effect, as he compares his experience to theirs: Count me out of your fantastic heavenly fellowship, for my ministry has to a large extent been hell on earth! In contrast to your wisdom, privilege, and power, I have experienced foolishness, disrepute, weakness, hunger, nakedness, homelessness, exhaustion, and persecution. Indeed, I and my fellow apostles are nothing but riffraff and rubbish, the scum of the earth (1 Cor. 4:10-13). We are like criminals condemned to die while the universe watches the spectacle in the amphitheater of this world (4:9). "Would to God that you did reign so we might reign with you, O great Corinthians" (4:8, paraphrase), but our vocation is to suffer for the sake of Christ (4:10). Paul's connection with Jesus in His suffering is strengthened when he uses the example and teaching of Jesus to characterize his ministry: "When reviled we bless; when persecuted we endure, when slandered we speak kindly" (4:12, 13; see also Luke 23:24; 6:28; 1 Pet. 2:21, 23).

Thus, Paul describes his ministry in terms befitting the crucified Christ. It was the crucified Christ he preached, and the crucified Christ he experienced in his life and ministry. He fervently believed that God's power was made perfect in weakness, not in the wisdom and strength of men (2 Cor. 12:9). He says, " I am content with weaknesses, insults, hardships, persecutions . . . for the sake of Christ; for whenever I am weak, then I am strong" (12:10). Denying all self-sufficiency, he carried the image of the dying Saviour in his body so that the life of Jesus might be manifested there for the sake of his converts (2 Cor. 4:10-12).

Paul wanted the Corinthians to take their cue from him and realize that now is not the time for living in glory, but for bearing the cross in imitation of Christ. Let the Corinthians re-evaluate themselves, not in terms of worldly norms of religious excellence, but in terms of the Cross with its message of self-giving, caring love and servanthood. The same re-evaluation awaits us as well.

Paul the spiritual father

With 1 Corinthians 4:13, Paul closes the discussion about idolizing leaders and fomenting disunity, but the issue of his authority still remained. From 1:10 to 4:13 Paul admonished the Corinthians not to make him the authority they did, but commencing with 4:14, he asks for recognition of the authority he really does have as Christ's apostle and their spiritual father.

When Paul says he did not want to make his converts ashamed (4:14), is he talking in an absolute sense? The Corinthians should have been ashamed of some of their attitudes and actions! A few tears would have been a good sign. In any case, what Paul wanted to create was not primarily shame, but an understanding which would change their lives. The past has already been lived. The future needs a different direction. So Paul says his purpose has been to admonish and correct them, as a caring father would his children. This is an enviable goal for any instructor or counselor.

In 4:13-21 Paul sees himself as a parent. He asserts that they may have countless guardians in Christ, like Apollos and others, but he was their only father, because he had brought the church into being through preaching the gospel (4:15). Because he was their father, he was sending them their brother, Timothy, who was a "beloved child" as they were "beloved children" (4:14). But Timothy was also "faithful," something a significant number of them could not claim. Because Timothy was faithful, he would be able to remind them, by his speech and demeanor, of Paul's ways, not his ways in general, but his "ways in Christ Jesus" (4:17). Timothy was to hold up before the Corinthian church their father, Paul, as a model of faith and action so his Corinthian children could imitate him (4:16).

Because he frequently calls for imitation (1 Cor. 11:1; 1 Thess. 1:6; 2:14; 2 Thess. 3:7-9; Gal. 4:2; Phil. 3:17; 4:9), critics have accused Paul of an exaggerated ego. This misunderstands him. Pagans, who had never seen or heard of Christianity, needed models. This is also true today. People, especially the young, need models who are transparent and accessible. The key is what Paul says in 1 Corinthians 10:33-11:1: "not seeking my own advantage, but that of the many, so that they may be saved. Be imitators of me as I am of Christ." The call to imitate Paul is really a challenge to follow Christ, rather than one's own advantage, and to work for the salvation of all. Teachers who only talk, but do not embody their teachings in actions are of no help whatever; they hinder moral development. I once read a newspaper article in which an ethics teacher decried the fact that his students expected him to live ethically since he taught ethics. He objected: "I'm only an ethics *teacher*; they shouldn't expect me to live that way!" But of Jesus it has been said so beautifully: "Not only did He teach the truth, but He was the truth. It was this that gave His teaching power" (*Education*, 79).

Tough love

In the Roman world, of which Corinth was a colony, a father had absolute authority over his children. He could, if he wished, scourge, imprison, or even kill them. In Corinthians Paul redefines the role of a father as that of a suffering servant, one who would do or go through anything to be able to impart the wisdom of the Cross to his children.

In verse 18 Paul's fatherly tone changes as he thinks of some of his outspoken, arrogant children in Corinth. They were giving other church members the impression that Paul had put his tail between his legs and run off, afraid to return and face the music of congregational criticism. Their attitude, betraying a spirit of opposition in the church, got Paul's dander up. A father's gentle love now turns to tough love. With undoubtedly strong emotion, Paul says that his soon return is certain if the Lord wills. He wants to deal with the unruly rascals who are challenging him, their spiritual father, but all of his plans are in the Lord's hand. And, as we learn from 1 Corinthians 16:9, 10, the Lord wanted him to stay in Ephesus, where he had gone after Corinth, because a door for evangelism had opened and adversaries were thick. Nevertheless, when he came back to Corinth, he intended to call his adversaries' bluff. He would see if their challenge was anything more than hot air, for the kingdom of God depends not on talk but on power (4:19). Power? He would show them who had real power! Take your pick, he challenged with fatherly authority, shall I come to you with a rod of discipline, or with loving gentleness?

One thing is for sure, Paul was not going to sit idly by and let his work for God evaporate by allowing destructive insinuations to abound and his converts to just do their own thing. Ministers and church leaders need to awake to their duty not only to evangelize and nurture, but also to speak firmly and discipline where necessary. "Spare the rod and spoil the church" is sometimes true.

Our choice

Just as the Corinthians had to make a choice as to how they wished Paul to relate to them, with gentleness or severity, so we have a choice as to how we want God to relate to us, with grace or judgment. God longs to speak graciously to us in seeking our improvement. After all, "God so loved the world" (John 3:16). Because of His love, He wishes for humble, open children, who are willing to put away their suspicions of Him, their own egos and self-interests, to listen to His word and follow in His way. If pride goes before a fall, genuine humility can be the basis for God's grace to work restoration in us. "For the grace of God has appeared, bringing salvation to all, training us to renounce impiety and worldly passions, and in the present age to live lives that are self-controlled, upright, and godly, while we wait for the blessed hope and the manifestation of the glory of our great God and Savior, Jesus Christ (Titus 2:11-13).

*Before we let the tough teachings of Jesus die the death of a
thousand qualifications, we need to let them penetrate our
hearts and minds and hit us in our moral solar plexus.*

Chapter 5

1 Corinthians 5:1–6:8

LAWLESS MORALITY AND IMMORAL LEGALITY

False judgments and true

In chapters 1-4 of 1 Corinthians Paul spoke about the church
not making false judgments—about wisdom, Christian life, and
leadership. Now he flips the coin and begins to discuss the subject of the church making true judgments. He maintains that
the church must be careful about judging its leaders when they
are acting as its servants, but it is called to take action against
activities inimical to the life of the community (5:1-13). At the
same time, believers must not be involved in irresponsible, secular judgments against fellow believers, for this would be sup-
porting unChristian behavior in the life of the church itself (6:1-
8). Thus, chapter 5 deals with the exercise of judicial process
among fellow believers, as a part of church discipline, and 6:1-
8 is concerned with judicial proceedings against fellow believers as a part of secular adjudication.

Arrogant immorality

So often what threatens to pollute the church's life comes
from the outside—from peers, political structures, and culture.
But in 1 Corinthians 5 the source of pollution comes from within
the church itself. Paul is shocked because reports are floating
about that the Christian community is tolerating behavior that
is almost unheard of, even among pagans. A man was living in
a sexual relationship with his father's wife. This violated the
convictions of the moral writers of the Greco-Roman world and

was completely opposed to Old Testament teachings which decried such unions (Deut. 22:30; Lev. 18:8). In Scripture a curse was even placed upon it: "Cursed be anyone who lies with his father's wife, because he has violated his father's rights" (Deut. 27:20).

The woman was undoubtedly not the man's mother, or she would have been called such. She was his stepmother. She also was not a Christian or Paul would have asked for her removal from the church as well as the man's (1 Cor. 5:2, 5, 13). The father may have died or divorced her, but a son just does not cohabit with his father's sexual partner. It defies Scripture, reason, and custom.

What would have sparked such behavior on the part of the man and the attitude of the church in allowing it? Why was the church arrogant about the whole matter rather than grieving and doing something about it (5:2)? It is difficult to believe that in Paul's eighteen-month sojourn in Corinth he did not offer counsel on sexual morality. He knew how licentious the pagan culture was, and that his converts would need to be educated about sanctification and sex (1 Thess. 4:1-8). Furthermore, knowledge of this need had already led him to give written counsel against association with immoral persons (1 Cor. 5:9). It is obvious that the unremorseful Corinthians had not taken his advice to heart. Their "superior wisdom" had led them to condone and perhaps even foster the presence of immorality in the congregation. Why? We could mention such things as the fact that their society was patriarchal, and "boys will be boys." (In a double-standard society, you would never hear, "girls will be girls"!) But this won't help for, as 5:1 says, even the pagans were against what would have been seen as an incestuous union. Possibly, if the woman was wealthy, the man might not have wanted her money to pass to another family, or if he was wealthy, the church might be losing a rich donor by acting against him. As today, so then: "Money talks."

False freedom

I believe a deeper reason was involved, however, and its foundation was theology. As we have seen previously, the Corinthians felt their resurrection had already occurred, that they had been filled with wisdom, the Spirit, and power, and had been transformed into spiritual beings who did not have to worry about sin or the flesh anymore. In a spiritual sense they thought they had already been glorified. They may have thought that allowing the man to live with his father's wife demonstrated their newfound freedom and the lawfulness of all things (6:12). In the second century A. D., certain Gnostic Christians engaged in licentiousness to prove they were free from the flesh. The Corinthian attitude may have been the same. That's why they were haughty about the whole matter. "So what, who cares?" or even, "Three cheers" was their stance. It reminds me of Romans 1:32, where Paul shows just how low humanity can go: "They know God's decree, that those who do such things deserve to die—yet they not only do them but even applaud others who practice them."

It is a paradoxical truth: When we think we are really high, we may actually be low. When we estimate ourselves to be low, we may truly be high. As the servant of the Lord says, "The closer you come to Jesus, the more faulty you will appear in your own eyes; for your vision will be clearer" (*Steps to Christ,* 64). This does not mean we are getting worse on the moral level, but that Christ is arousing us, shaping and deepening our character to be like His.

Since the "professionals" in wisdom were doing nothing about purifying their congregational life and were indifferent to Paul's authority, Paul decided to take the matter in hand. Did he ever! There is such a thing as destroying the church (1 Cor. 3:16, 17), and Paul, as an apostle and the father of this church, was not going to let that happen.

Exercising judgment

The prophets dealt with judgment, and Paul was about to make a prophetic judgment. He solemnly intones: "For though absent in the body, I am present in spirit; and as if present I have already pronounced judgment in the name of the Lord Jesus on the man who has done such a thing" (5:3, 4). Paul was physically in Ephesus, but in a spiritual sense he was in Corinth.

He was there because the Holy Spirit who called him to service and gave him power to carry it on (see 2:4) was there, and because his voice was being heard as his letter was read to the congregation. When your mother or father writes you a letter, don't you feel their presence as you read their words?

Paul declares that as an authoritative apostle and prophetic voice, he has already pronounced judgment on the perpetrator of the incestuous liaison. He may sound cold and hard here, but as we shall see, he has a saving intention in mind. Since Paul, like a judge, has rendered the verdict, he now calls upon the congregation to execute it. This was in accord with Jesus' teaching that the church had the authority and responsibility to make decisions about church discipline (Matt. 18:15-18).

Redemptive discipline

Paul specifies what the congregation should do when it convenes with a sense of his presence and the power of the Lord Jesus. It is in Jesus' name that Paul pronounces judgment, and it is with Jesus' power that the community is to execute judgment (1 Cor. 5:3, 4). Paul directs the church to "hand over this man to Satan for the destruction of the flesh" (5:5; compare 1 Tim. 1:20). Have you ever heard of such a dire directive? Why, in the name of Jesus, would believers hand a sinner over to Satan? Did not Jesus come to save sinners? If Paul, as a murderous persecutor of God's people, could receive mercy (1 Tim. 1:13-16), could not this man as well? The answer is yes, and verse five proves it.

However, we must first get a picture of the world of thought involved in the handing over of the offender to Satan. Paul operated with an apocalyptic view of the world. The word apocalyptic comes from a word which means to reveal. In the apocalyptic understanding of things, like that in the books of Daniel and Revelation, this world is dominated by Satan as its god or ruler (2 Cor. 4:4; John 14:30; 16:11). But within this enslaved world is an island of refuge and strength, the church of Jesus Christ, against which the gates of hell shall not prevail (Matt. 16:18). To be in the church is to be in God's territory. To be outside is to be in Satan's domain. This is where handing over or excommunication brings a person.

Paul says that the immediate purpose for sending the man into Satan's realm is to bring about the destruction of the man's flesh. This sounds more ominous than ever. Is Paul talking about the man's physical body? Does he want the man to become ill or die as some did who desecrated the Lord's Supper (1 Cor. 11:30)? This cannot be Paul's meaning because it would totally contradict the ending of verse five. But what about that awful sounding phrase "the destruction of the flesh"? As mentioned before, "flesh" stands most often in Paul's writings for man's sinful inclinations. When you read in Galatians 5:24: "And those who belong to Christ Jesus have crucified the flesh with its passions and desires," does that sound dreadful or desirable? And when Romans 6:6 speaks about the old self being crucified so that sin's domination over the body "might be destroyed," does that seem terrible? "Not at all," you say. Well, that's Paul's point in 1 Corinthians 5:5. By sending the man from the security, protection, and encouragement of the church to a place of insecurity, anxiety, and fear, Paul hopes for an awakening of conscience, repentance, and the man's return to the church. It is like the parable of the prodigal son. He left home and squandered his life in riotous living but, "when he came to himself" (Luke 15:17). That's it! Sin has been a kind of insanity, but as with Alcoholics Anonymous and other Twelve Step plans, when a person hits rock bottom, which is the first step, the way is prepared for taking the giant leap of the second step—looking to a power higher than themselves. As in the parable, in the pigpen of life (Satan's domain) the person comes to himself and says: "I will get up and go to my father."

That is what Paul wishes for the man in the Corinthian church. Filled with the remorse he and the church should have had, instead of the arrogance they did have, he would see that Satan's ground is no place for him to be, but the church, where the Holy Spirit dwells, is. This is "the destruction of the flesh."

Terminating "the flesh" is the immediate purpose of the expulsion, but the ultimate purpose is the main point of the text: "so that his spirit might be saved in the day of the Lord" (1 Cor. 5:5). Paul was not a dualist like the Greeks. For him, "flesh" and "spirit" designate not two parts of a person, the Greek view, but the whole person oriented either toward self and sin, ("flesh") or toward God and His will ("Spirit"). When the day of the Lord comes, Paul does not want to see the man lost, but saved.

Besides the ultimate salvation of the sinner, there is another reason why disfellowshiping may sometimes be necessary—the preservation of the church. Paul says that a little leaven leavens the whole lump (5:7). The tentacles of blatant immorality, if unchecked, may reach deeper into the church's life and affect the whole. The old leaven of evil has to be cast out because Christ, the Passover Lamb, has already been sacrificed and believers have already become new loaves of unleavened bread. In other words, Christ's death has created a transformed people. Therefore, the time has long since passed when "the yeast of malice and evil" should be present, but the time has come for the "unleavened bread of sincerity and truth" (5:8). "Truth," as the opposite of evil, stands for a course of life that comports with the crucified Christ, not just an abstract belief system.

Thus, the church can only be itself when it stands against evil, while at the same time, as in verse five, seeking to reclaim those under its influence. The question remains for us to answer today: In our discipline can we be truly redemptive, yet decidedly opposed to evil? This twofold task of the church is illustrated in the following incidents.

I remember visiting a church years ago where a person who had an illegitimate child was seated toward the front of the sanctuary. Several rows behind were two people discussing the presence in church of one who had committed such a wrong. I was seated directly behind and could not help but overhear what they were saying. I thought to myself: *Where is the great sin here, with the one who in sorrow had returned to the church to find life, or with the persons who had no redemptive interest in one who had slipped?* To me, reflection on what God's greatest gift is leads to a conclusion about what the greatest sin must be. Since that gift is God's compassionate love, the greatest sin must be the absence of caring love and compassion.

But here is another kind of story. I visited a large church

where the pastor brought to my attention the presence of a man who had been visiting several women at the same time, sweet-talking them and leading them into physical intimacy. None of the women knew about the others. Each one thought she was being courted by the man, and the only one receiving his attentions. But the cat jumped out of the bag, and the multiple affairs became known to all the women, and others as well. It was a sorry and hurtful mess indeed. How should it be handled? When the pastor had the first inkling of what was happening, the perpetrator was visited and confronted. However, he did not repent and desist. In such a situation only one thing can be done. As unfortunate as it is, such a person has to be expelled before the honor of the church, its witness to Christ, and the spiritual and emotional health of its members are severely impaired. Paul taught that association with church members whose lifestyles betray shameless disregard of the church's standards should be avoided (5:9, 11) and corporate discipline should be administered (5:13). But again let us emphasize, because it can be forgotten so easily: the gospel demands that we make the purpose of present judgment the final redemption of the individual.

Shame on you

If the church is called by God to exercise judgment, as 5:1-13 shows, wouldn't that mean that the church has the resources for dealing with problems in its life without recourse to secular courts? You would think so. But the Corinthians did not see this. In contradiction to their refusal to judge immorality in their midst, they were seeking legal judgments against each other, sometimes with immoral intent. Christians were hauling one another into court before unrighteous (unbelieving) judges, not only to settle disputes but even to defraud fellow church members.

The only word to describe Paul's feelings about God's people going to the world to settle issues between Christians is "horror." In a question that is actually an exclamation, he says: "How dare you!" Their actions are inconceivable! Whatever happened to all that wisdom the Corinthians claimed to have?

This issue is not only about who Christians *are*—God's people, possessing His spirit, and motivated by Christ's Gospel—but about what Christians have been called to *do* at the time of the final judgment. Christians are going to judge the world (6:2)! This includes the very judges they now are appealing to! But beyond this, they will even be judging angels as well! How then can they be incompetent in the present to settle trivial cases of "brother with brother" (6:3, 6)? The Corinthians made much of the "wise." OK, says Paul in biting sarcasm, is there no one wise enough among you to settle such disputes (6:5)? Whereas Paul did not wish to shame the Corinthians over the issue of cliques (4:14), he did want them to feel shame over this issue which affected the church's being and witness (6:6).

But Paul's argument has not yet reached its highest point. Even apart from considerations as to who should settle legal matters, Paul wonders why there are lawsuits among believers in the first place. "That is already a defeat for you," he asserts (6:7). Then, in the spirit of Jesus, he probingly asks: "Why not rather be wronged? Why not rather be defrauded?" (6:7).

Some may think this is a call to be a royal doormat. Wrong! Taking into view verse 8, where Paul charges, "But you yourselves wrong and defraud," his meaning must be: "Why not rather be willing to be defrauded than to defraud?" If these are the two alternatives, the Christian's choice is clear. A person living in Christ, who all the way to the cross gave up his rights so he could save others (Phil. 2:6-8) would always much rather take the wrong than do the wrong. Besides, doing wrong to others disqualifies one from God's kingdom (1 Cor. 6:9), which is built upon the principles of love and service.

The issue is whether we are willing to follow the crucified Jesus in every area of our lives. God does not call us to be doormats, but to be like Jesus. Before we let the tough teachings of Jesus die the death of a thousand qualifications, we need to let them penetrate our hearts and minds and hit us in our moral solar plexus. After we have felt the full force of his revolutionary call to be the meek and merciful, the reconciled and reconcilers, then we can allow questions about application and just how to best fulfill our Christian calling in difficult situations. Years ago, Charles Sheldon's book, *In His Steps*, appeared. It summoned us, as Christ's followers, to seriously ask ourselves in every problematical situation, "What would Jesus do?" We need to act and be like Him. The goal of every believer is simply and beautifully expressed in the words we sing:

> Be like Jesus, this my song,
> In the home and in the throng.
> Be like Jesus all day long!
> I would be like Jesus.
> *Seventh-day Adventist Hymnal*, #311

God is mocked when we make His expensive grace, the sacrifice of His Son for us, into cheap grace . . . as if [He] did not care how we live our lives after receiving His gift of eternal life.

Chapter 6

1 Corinthians 6:9-20

SEX AND SANCTIFICATION

A deception unmasked

In 1 Corinthians 6:1-8 it may seem that Paul is hard on the righteous and soft on wrongdoers when he challenges believers not to engage in lawsuits but rather to let themselves be wronged and defrauded (6:7). However, he now takes up the other side of the coin and solemnly asks: "Do you not know that wrongdoers will not inherit the kingdom of God" (6:9)? Believers may be called to turn the other cheek by suffering wrong, but they should rest assured that God will not let those who persist in wrongdoing off the hook. They will be judged. Elsewhere Paul puts it this way: "If it is possible, so far as it depends on you, live peaceably with all. Beloved, never avenge yourselves, but leave room for the wrath of God; for it is written, 'Vengeance is mine, I will repay, says the Lord' " (Rom. 12:18, 19). Injustice will never escape God's judgment, and fairness will ultimately prevail. According to the apostle Peter, believers are called to follow Jesus' example in the face of wrong treatment. He never returned evil for evil, but entrusted himself to God who judges justly (1 Pet. 2:21, 23). God is the final court of appeal, and we can trust Him to act in favor of His people.

Why does Paul say, "Do you not know?" meaning, "Surely you are aware," and then, "Do not be deceived" (6:9)? Do the Corinthians know or not? They must have heard about the judgment when Paul taught them the gospel, but their view of themselves made it easy to not take such instruction seriously and personally. They seem to have thought: "We are God's special, enlightened, spiritual people; surely we are beyond judgment!"

They had an easy security that did not take seriously the fact that God expects responsible, holy conduct from His still-temptable people. This is where Christians—especially those who believe in the gospel teaching of righteousness by faith—can be deceived. Being justified by faith does not mean we can continue in evil works.

It is significant how many times Paul expresses his concern over this matter. In Colossians 3:5, 6 he lists a number of evils and then says: "On account of these the wrath of God is coming." According to 1 Thessalonians 4:6, God is an avenger with respect to evil "as we . . . solemnly forewarned you." No cheap grace with Paul! God expects change and makes change possible. In Galatians 5:21 Paul introduces a list of vices that block access to God's kingdom with the words, "I am warning you, as I warned you before." Though sounding negative, this warning is there to preserve God's people from living contrary to salvation and denying what it means to be Christian. One of Paul's strongest warnings comes in Ephesians 5:5, 6: "*Be sure of this*, that no fornicator . . . or one who is greedy . . . has any inheritance in the kingdom of Christ and of God. *Let no one deceive you* with empty words" (emphasis supplied). In Galatians 6:7 not being deceived is coupled with the thought: "*God is not mocked*, for you reap whatever you sow" (emphasis supplied). God is mocked when we make His expensive grace, the sacrifice of His Son for us, into cheap grace, in which there is heard no call to repentance, obedience, and discipleship—as if God did not care how we live our lives after receiving His gift of eternal life.

Dietrich Bonhoeffer, the German pastor executed for his resistance to Hitler's evil regime during World War II, movingly wrote about this in his book, *The Cost of Discipleship*. It cost God much to save us, and it cost Bonhoeffer his life to be a faithful witness. To the end, he bore not merely the message of forgiveness but the cross itself, the emblem of servanthood and self-giving. Jesus said, "Take up your cross and follow me."

Bonhoeffer perseveringly did, and we must also.

Jeremiah 7:8-10 exposes the mocking contradiction between grace received for salvation but denied in the life: "Behold, you trust in deceptive words to no avail. Will you steal, murder, commit adultery, swear falsely . . . and then come and stand before me in this house, which is called by my name, and say, 'We are delivered'—only to go on doing all these abominations?" (RSV).

In my distant memory I recall an old Adventist poem that makes the same point. The beginning and ending of it go something like this:

> Free from the law
> O happy condition!
> I can sin all I want
> and still claim remission.
>
> Nothing in the law
> has any claim on me,
> for I'm saved by grace
> and entirely free.
>
> So let's all beware
> of that Adventist creed
> that it's grace producing obedience
> that all of us need.

Christianity spells change

After giving an expanded list of the kinds of persons and lifestyles God does not approve, Paul says, "And this is what some of you used to be. But you were washed, you were sanctified, you were justified" (1 Cor. 6:11). Paul is glad for the decided change the gospel brings. People who were unclean become pure (washed), persons who had lived for themselves are now set apart for God and His service (sanctification), and those who were unrighteous come into a right relationship with God (justification). This had happened among the Corinthians, but some of them, embracing a "once saved, always saved, no matter what I do" mentality, were in danger of misunderstanding or forgetting the new moral life to which Christ had called them.

Fornication pro and con

An outstanding illustration of this was the attitude of some with respect to fornication. In their culture, the purpose of wives was understood as caring for the home and bearing children. Visiting prostitutes was considered a normal way for husbands—but not their wives—to find sexual pleasure. A double standard with a vengeance! Remarkably, certain Corinthian Christians found no incompatibility between pagan customs and their conversion to Christ. They were frequenting prostitutes with impunity, and had arguments to support their actions. The first was represented by their slogan, twice repeated by Paul—"All things are lawful" (6:12). They had picked up the note of freedom in Paul's gospel and driven it right into the ground. Instead of freedom *from* sin and freedom *for* righteousness, they took freedom in an absolute sense, as making everything permissible. This was especially the case for those who believed that their exalted, enlightened spiritual state guaranteed they could no longer be touched by sin in their inner, transformed selves. Since their bodily lives could not affect their spiritual lives, why not visit harlots? It was harmless, and perhaps even helpful for demonstrating just how free their inner selves were from any fleshly influences. There is evidence from the second century that certain "Christian" Gnostics (those who claimed they had special, esoteric knowledge that guaranteed escape from the fleshly to the spiritual realm) deliberately engaged in licentiousness to prove how free they were. Paul has advice for anyone, ancient or modern, who fits this description: "For you were called to freedom, brethren; only do not use your freedom as an opportunity for the flesh" (Gal. 5:13, RSV).

Paul's answer to this argument about lawfulness was twofold (1 Cor. 6:12). First, the real issue was not whether something was lawful on esoteric grounds, but whether it was *beneficial* in everyday life. Paul was clear that there are things which could never be helpful, only hurtful (6:18). Second, using a play on words, he argued that the question was not whether I have authority to do anything I want but whether anything should have the authority to do what it wants with me! A misuse of sexuality can dominate a person. I may become a slave to my freedom and, paradoxically, fall under the control of what I feel free to do. Pornography, for example, can become a serious addiction, adversely affecting one's perception of personhood and his or her social interactions, particularly within marital and family life.

Another Corinthian argument had to do with the naturalness of all things, including fornication. Their reasoning was simple: Foods for the belly and the belly for foods (6:13). They argued that just as the belly and foods were fitted for each other, so the sexual organs were created to be joined with someone—and prostitutes were ready-made for that. So, "Do what comes naturally!" How modern this argument is! Today we hear: "What's wrong with it? Just having a little fun. Besides, everyone's doing it."

Paul refutes this by maintaining that the eating analogy does not fit the sexual reality. What happens when the body digests food is not the same as what happens when the body engages in fornication. Sex, which expresses and fosters an intimate relationship between two people, is a function of the whole person in a way that eating is not. This whole person is meant for the Lord, not for fornication. Using the body for the Lord in His service is the appropriate response to the fact that the Lord has been for the body by acting for its salvation. The adage, "One for all, and all for one" expresses the principle involved, but it should be understood as "Christ for all, and all for Christ."

The Corinthian's third argument for the legitimacy of fornication was found in eschatology. Thinking that the stomach and food illustrated the relation between the body and sex, their position was: "God will destroy both one and the other" (6:13). Because the Greeks believed in the immortality of the soul, they thought the body would one day be destroyed and the soul released. If the body had no permanent destiny, what difference did it make what one did with it?

Paul's answer was that it makes a big difference when you

understand the destiny of the body. His thinking is clarified
when compared with what they said (6:13, 14):

Corinthians	Paul
Stomach for food	Body not for fornication but for the Lord
food for the stomach	and the Lord for the body
God will destory the one	God raised the Lord
and the other	and will raise us by His power

This comparison shows that according to Paul the body is
not a transient reality, but has an eternal destiny. It will be
raised up just as was the body of Jesus. The lesson is clear: If,
in our body, we are destined to live eternally with the risen
Lord, that should affect how we treat our body in this world.
Life, which will one day be fulfilled with Christ, should not
now be filled with sin. Our future destiny reveals our present
duty.

Belonging to Christ and sexual promiscuity
Furthering his argument as to why fornication is wrong, Paul
speaks of the relationship between the bodies (persons) of the
Corinthians and the risen Christ. They should realize that their
bodies are members of the risen Christ. Here is the beginning
of the idea that Christ is our head and we are His body (12:27;
Col. 1:18, 24). Being the property of Christ is totally incompat-
ible with being partners with prostitutes. Paul calls on Genesis 2:24, originally describing the marriage union, to represent what happens in relations with prostitutes (6:16). *Sex is
never casual*; it forms a bond, whether good, as in marriage, or
bad, as in fornication. Sex, designed by God to forge and express physical and spiritual union with one's marital partner,
can also form an illegitimate, prostituting union which destroys
the spiritual union with the risen Christ (6:17).
That is why Paul directs that we "shun fornication" (6:18). It
is a sin directly against one's body, removing it from the spiritual union with Christ, which is the assurance of the future
resurrection of the body. As Paul says later, it is only "in Christ"

that all shall be made alive (15:22). Someone might take up the slogan, "Every sin is outside the body," meaning "Nothing really affects me," but Paul resoundingly replies, "Fornication does!" (6:18).

Not only does the body belong to Christ, but it is the dwelling place of the Holy Spirit (6:19). As such it should never be desecrated by unholy deeds. The presence of the Spirit testifies that we belong to Christ, rather than to ourselves (Rom 8:9; 1 Cor. 6:19). This belonging is very expensive—it took the purchase price of the death of Christ. That is why we are so urgently charged: "Glorify God in your body" (6:20).

The gospel, sex, and fornication

First Corinthians 6:12-20 leads us to some profound conclusions. First, the right use of human sexuality is very important to God and must be understood in the light of the gospel. Though the gospel ultimately concerns eternal life, it profoundly affects this life as well. Note the big gospel guns Paul uses to discuss sexuality:

1. Christ's death for us (implied in "for the body" in verse 13 and "purchased with a price" in verse 20);
2. Christ's resurrection from the dead and the future resurrection of all believers (verse 14);
3. The concept of the body of Christ, of which all believers are a part (verse 16);
4. union with God (verse 16);
5. the presence of the Holy Spirit in the life (verse 19).

How many of us would have thought that these central gospel truths had relevance not only for theology but also for our sexual lives? But they do! There is no element of our lives the gospel does not touch.

Second, the promiscuous sexuality and fornication that are taken for granted in contemporary society are contrary to the will of God. The Bible uses the word fornication as a general term for sexual immorality (for example Gal. 5:19; Col. 3:5) or specifically for relations with prostitutes (1 Cor. 6:12-20), incest (1 Cor. 5:1, 2; and Lev. 18:6-18), or adultery (Jer. 3:8; Hos. 2:2; Amos 7:17; Rev. 2:21, 22). If we want to know when fornication is present, these usages should be recalled. In addition, I would like to suggest some general principles which may be helpful.

Fornication is present when
1. Sex is separated from love, and eros (self-satisfaction) from agape (self-giving);
2. Means are separated from ends, sexual functions from personal relationships, and parts from persons;
3. Pleasure and fun are separated from responsibility and commitment;
4. A temporary sexual union is separated from a lifelong union of love;
5. Culture is separated from Christ, and the mores of the old life outside of Christ are separated from the morals of the new life in Christ;
6. Human proclivity is separated from divine principle, and decisions of human will are reached without seeking God's will.

Fornication is no superficial matter. It has profound significance for the meaning of persons and touches the central core of our being. Two stories will illustrate the great effect this misdirection of our sexuality can have on our lives.

As a young person, I lived for a time in New York City. One day I came across a newspaper account of the famous evangelist Billy Graham visiting a porno shop in the city. He didn't go there to peruse the offerings of the place but to offer the gospel of Jesus and its life-changing power. In my youthful enthusiasm I figured that if Billy Graham could do it, I could too! So with religious fervor and a degree of curiosity, I entered one of the many shops found in that city. I was unprepared for what I saw. I was struck by the many well-dressed men with briefcases—a business clientele to be sure—standing before a large section of magazines, looking neither right nor left, but busily flicking through the pages and gazing at the contents. In one corner of the room, on a raised platform, where he could be seen and heard best, was a hawker—a person who kept up an endless series of loud, rapid-fire sales pitches in an effort to get the browsers to buy. Sales seemed brisk that day. Mustering my courage, I approached the magazines to see what all the fuss was about. I was shocked. The pages of the magazines portrayed no faces, almost never a whole body, but only close-ups of body parts. Persons had vanished, and all that was left were mere body parts with only mechanical functions.

In such situations the image of God is not only defaced but erased, the concept of a "human being" is voided of all meaning, and love is surrendered for lust. You can only love a person, not a part.

Years later, I experienced an incident which reflects the logical outcome of this kind of mentality. I received a frantic call from a distraught mother. "Could you please go and check on my daughter. I think she's going to kill herself!" I went immediately. I urgently knocked on the front door, but there was no response. I found that the door was unlocked, and slowly entered the front room, but saw no one. As I moved further into the house, I saw an open bedroom door. I approached and timidly looked in. There she was, lying on the bed with her eyes closed and shaking violently. She had taken a large number of Valium tablets, but instead of producing tranquillity, their effect was the complete opposite. Realizing that her life was in extreme jeopardy, I called for one of her close friends, a nurse, and for an ambulance. She was rushed to the hospital where she received good care and, by God's grace, survived.

When she recovered, she told me the story of what had driven her to the extremity of suicide. Unhappily, her first marriage had ended. Later, she began to date, but her experiences with a number of men were not good. They seemed to have only one thing in mind. On one occasion, a man literally chased her around her own home in a fit of sexual desire. Her commentary on this, which spoke not only of him but others as well, was very telling: "They wanted something from me, but they didn't want me!"

How demeaning to personality and personhood and how contrary to the divine purpose for our wholeness and happiness. Our sexuality has been given us by God, not to selfishly focus upon our own gratification, but to minister to another in a mutual relationship of respect, self-giving love, and permanent commitment. This is where true joy may be found. Anything less than this is fornication, which at rock bottom is the misuse of another person and ourselves as well. As Christians, we are to rise above culture and glorify God with our body (1 Cor. 6:20).

The purpose of Paul's warfare against fornication in this chapter is not to deprive anyone of total fulfillment but to foster it. God wants to separate us from anything that diminishes or destroys our dignity in His image so that we can have the abundant life He has planned for us. This was the very purpose of the Incarnation, as Jesus Himself said: "I am come that they might have life, and that they might have it more abundantly" (John 10:10, KJV).

The ultimate focus of marriage should be the strengthening of our certainty of entering God's kingdom when Jesus comes. . . . The essence of the sexual relationship is self-giving love. Each partner is to minister to the other.

Chapter 7

1 Corinthians 7

SEXUALITY AND SPIRITUALITY

Sexuality and spirituality

When a wall is erected between the spiritual and physical realms, between spirit and flesh, and the spiritual categories are considered good and the material inferior or bad, two results for how people conduct their lives may follow. On the one hand, a libertine track can be pursued in which the fleshly way is followed with abandon since, it is believed, what happens in the body does not affect the spiritual self. We have seen an example of this in 1 Corinthians 6:12-20. On the other hand, one can follow an ascetic way of life in which the body's needs are denied rather than affirmed. There is a striking illustration of this in 1 Corinthians 7. How could anyone effectively pastor a church in which one group advocated free sex, and the other no sex! That was the situation in Corinth.

According to 1 Corinthians 7:1, the congregation had sent Paul a letter dealing with the topics covered in chapter 7. It is not certain whether their letter contained position statements, perhaps representing challenges to Paul, or if they were soliciting Paul's comments on their views and questions. In any case, it must be kept in mind when reading the chapter that Paul is evaluating *their* positions or answering *their* questions. Thus, he does not offer a complete or systematic presentation of his views, but says only what is necessary to respond to their concerns. To find out what they said or asked, we have to read between the lines of Paul's replies. When this is done, a dominant issue for 1 Corinthians 7 emerges: the relationship between sexuality and spirituality. It seems clear that the celibates of Corinth had opted for the view that sexuality and spirituality do not mix. If a person wants to be truly spiritual, the sexual has to go. Paul rebuts this position and exposes its dangers.

The celibacy position is well summarized in the lead statement of 1 Cor. 7:1: "It is well for a man not to touch a woman." Who said this, Paul or the Corinthians? More than likely it is a quote from their letter, for Paul immediately begins to show its inadequacy in the light of practical realities.

The ascetic wing of the Corinthian church undoubtedly applied the statement to marriage, for that is what Paul speaks of in verses 2-6. He shows how problematic this view is by declaring that if it were carried out, it might very well cause fornication. There were plenty of prostitutes in Corinth who could fulfill a person's sexual needs if they were not being fulfilled at home. Some have urged that Paul must have had a low view of married life to speak of it only in terms of a safeguard against fornication. After all, did he not say: "Because of the temptation to immorality, each man should have his own wife and each woman her own husband" (7:2, RSV)? But remember, Paul is here answering the church's statements in its letter to him and not trying to give the ultimate reason for marriage and sex. Rather he is stating the trouble people will be in if they try to live a celibate life when they do not have the gift of celibacy, spoken of in verse 7.

Paul goes on to discuss marital sex showing that its value is greater than just avoiding fornication. In verses 3-4 he specifies that a husband should give to his wife what is due her sexually, and likewise the wife to the husband. Marriage involves not only privileges but responsibilities. One of these is to minister to the sexual needs of one's partner (as also to the emotional, social, and spiritual needs). Since the two have become one, ministering to one's other half is also in effect ministering to one's self. Both partners' gifts are needed to supply wholeness to the lives of each. If there is to be an exception to sexual involvement as, for example, if the couple wishes to engage in a period of intense prayer and devotion, the decision to do so must be *mutual* and *temporary* (verse 5). Strict abstinence might weaken self-control and give Satan an opportunity to tempt to fornication. Abstention for prayer, however, is not a command, but only a concession by Paul (verse 6). Devotional life and sexual relationships can go together. In fact, the couple which prays together might have better sex together.

Paul's instruction in 7:2-6 is remarkable for a number of reasons. First, it is realistic in its understanding of the power of human sexuality, the need for regularity ("Do not deprive one another except . . ."), and the recognition that sex is not just for having children, but also for personal fulfillment. Second, it is based upon the principle of mutuality and equality. Contrary to what anyone might expect in Roman society, the man's duty to the woman is mentioned first (7:3), and the woman is said to have authority over (a legitimate interest in) his body as well as he over hers (7:4). Third, it is implied that the essence of the sexual relationship is self-giving love. Each partner is to minister to the other. These principles brought into today's world would revolutionize marital and sexual relations between couples. Paul certainly was not behind the times, nor was he anti-marriage or anti-sex, as certain critics have charged.

Paul does acknowledge that he wishes all were as himself, unmarried and self-contained, but he recognizes, as did Jesus, that celibacy takes a special gift from God (7:7; Matt. 19:10, 11).

He illustrates this in the case of unmarried people and widows (7:8, 9). While he might wish them to be as he is, he recognizes that some might not have the necessary inner controls. They should marry, he advocates, for marriage, in which one's drives can find legitimate satisfaction, is a much better choice than to be aflame with unrelieved passion. Once again, Paul is entirely realistic. He understands something about human nature. "Don't live a life unnatural to yourself" is his counsel.

So strong were the Corinthian champions for celibacy that they recommended divorce so one could escape the closeness that made sexual abstinence more difficult (7:10-16). Can you imagine giving up a lifelong partnership of love so that sex could be avoided! What is so wrong with sex? God could not have considered it wrong for, instead of creating sexless beings, he made humans male and female and declared that they should "cling" to each other, for they had become one flesh (Gen. 1:27; 2:24). Furthermore, he pronounced it all "very good" (Gen. 1:31). But an alien philosophy, contrary to Scripture, came in exalting spirit and devaluing matter. According to this view, the goal was to be rid of the flesh and its appetites and, through spiritual illumination, ascend to the pure realm of spirit above. Abstinence from sex was one major step on this path. An illustration of this ascetic view is found in 1 Timothy 4:3, where Paul describes last day heretics as forbidding marriage, with its sexual involvements, and demanding abstinence from certain foods.

Following this track of thought the Corinthians recommended divorce, even when both partners were Christian. Paul's response was to quote Jesus' teaching about the indissolubility of marriage (1 Cor. 7:9, 10; Mark 10:11, 12), and he applied the same principle to situations where one partner was a Christian and the other an unbeliever (pagan) (7:11-16). In harmony with Jesus' teaching the believer was to stay united to the unbeliever unless the unbeliever was intent on deserting the marriage. In that case, the believer was not bound to the marriage, for "it is to peace that God has called you" (7:15). Moreover, it is uncertain that one can do much to save a partner who is intent on deserting the marriage lock, stock, and barrel (7:16).

The Corinthians were not at all happy about the thought of staying with their unbelieving partners, for they were convinced that they and their children would become polluted by continued contact. Not so, says Paul, for the Christian sanctifies the non-Christian and the children as well (7:14). Light is stronger than darkness, belief than unbelief, Christianity than its opposite. This harmonizes with Jesus' teaching that His followers are to be salt and light to the world so that everyone might see the good works of God's people and glorify the Father in heaven (Matt. 5:13-16). Furthermore, Jesus was not afraid to touch lepers, for His healing power was stronger than their disease. Likewise, Christians should never be afraid to confront spiritual leprosy. That song is correct which says of believers: "Greater is he who is in you, than he who is in the world."

After recommending in 7:17-24 that Christians should remain in whatever state they were called, since social stratification has nothing to do with Christian identification—in Christ slaves become free, and the free become slaves (7:22)—Paul returns to the issue of marriage (7:25-40). In this section another reason is presented for staying as one is—the end of the world.

Paul asserts that both the married and the unmarried should stay as they are (7:25-27) because of the "impending crisis" (7:26). He will explain what he means by this, but first he lets the singles know that, while marriage is not at all wrong (7:28, 36), as certain ascetics in the church believed, he wants to spare them from the distresses married people have to go through (7:28). When Paul speaks of an "impending crisis" is he just talking about problems in general, or does he have something more specific in mind? Clearly the latter. Paul sets forth his reasoning in a truly great New Testament passage containing the essence of what it means to be an Adventist Christian. Paul has already spoken of "the imminent crisis." In spelling out what he means by this, he says, "the appointed time has grown short" (7:29) and "the present form of this world is passing away" (7:31). Without a doubt these expressions refer to the end of all things and the revelation of the Lord Jesus on the day when He will come again. It is for this that the Corinthians had already been waiting (1:7, 8). They and Paul were those "on whom the ends of the ages have come" (10:11). Paul pictured time as short, just as modern Adventists have. Ellen White was accused of falsehood because time had continued longer than her testimony had indicated. In response she asked if Christ and His disciples were deceived by the testimonies they bore as to the shortness of time in such texts as 1 Corinthians 7:29, 30; Romans 13:12; and Revelation 22:6, 7. Then she declared: "The angels of God in their messages to men represent time as very short" (*Selected Messages*, 1:67).

Paul teaches that the soon coming of Jesus should relativize all earthly values. He chooses several major areas of human experience: marriage, sadness, gladness, ownership, commerce and culture, and says with respect to each that, in view of the coming of Christ, they should not be seen as ultimate. Believers should treat each of these existing realities *as though* they did not really exist as primary concerns.

If you are married, be *as though* you were not. This cannot mean doing away with marriage since Paul has recommended it, denied divorce, and advocated that sex, equality, and mutuality should characterize it. The point is that as good as marriage is, it cannot compare with or replace the ultimate joy of Christ's return when everyone will be swept into His eternal fellowship. Earthly ties should not be made into idols, for the coming Christ alone is Lord.

If you mourn (and Paul says, "Weep with those who weep," Rom. 12:15), be *as though* not mourning, for Christ's coming will wipe away every tear. Tears are not the final truth for, at Christ's coming, the dead will rise. In view of that, present tears can be tears of joy. I agree with the tombstone inscription:

> Go home dear friends,
> dry your tears,
> We must wait here
> till Christ appears.

If you rejoice (and Paul says, "Rejoice with those who rejoice," Rom. 12:15), remember that nothing earth offers is comparable to "Enter into the joy of thy Lord."

If you buy, be *as though* you had no earthly possessions, for "what can be seen is temporary, but what cannot be seen is eternal" (2 Cor. 4:18). Jesus said: "Do not store up for yourselves treasures on earth, where moth and rust consume and where thieves break through and steal; but store up for yourselves treasures in heaven" (Matt. 6:19, 20).

If you deal with the world, utilizing its commerce and culture to achieve your goals, be *as though* you had no dealings with it, "for the present form of this world is passing away" (1 Cor. 7:31).

In other words, Christians are to put their supreme investment in what is yet to be with Christ, rather than with what presently is in the world. Paul's message is summarized in the song:

> Turn your eyes upon Jesus,
> Look full in His wonderful face;
> And the things of earth will grow strangely dim
> In the light of His glory and grace.
> —*Seventh-day Adventist Hymnal*, 290

Because Christ's coming is the focus of Christian existence, it supplies the reason for Paul seeing marriage as good but singleness as better (7:38), that is, as having a particular benefit during the last days (singleness is not intrinsically better). Paul is not an ascetic when he suggests that there is a benefit in remaining single (7:32-35). Those who are married must necessarily occupy themselves with many concerns, and Paul sees advantages in being able to devote oneself more fully to the work of the soon coming Lord rather than to the affairs of household and family. In saying this, Paul is not laying down a law. In his own words: "I say this for your own benefit, *not to put any restraint upon you*, but to promote good order and unhindered devotion to the Lord" (7:35, emphasis supplied).

How should contemporary Adventists react to this? The counsel of James and Ellen White, who spoke directly to this matter, is relevant here. Their advice, in the form of a question, not of a legal demand, was that if Paul could remain single and recommend it to others for the reasons given in 1 Corinthians 7, would it not be a commendable course today for people to remain unmarried unless evidences were unmistakable that, by marrying, they would be bettering their condition, and making heaven more sure? (*Advent Review and Sabbath Herald*, March 24, 1868). No better reasons for marriage during the difficult last days can be given. Here is instruction which fits the spirit of the great Second Advent passage in 7:29-31. That passage specified that the focus of our lives should be the coming King and His kingdom. Here it is said that beyond the consideration of bettering our human condition, the ultimate focus of marriage should be the strengthening of our certainty of entering God's kingdom when Jesus comes. If this advice were followed, both marriage and our prospects for heaven would be more permanent. Each partner, with eyes fixed on Christ, could aid and abet the other in a deeper life of prayer, more fervent study of Scripture, a closer walk with God, more dedicated service to others, and thus a more earnest preparation for Jesus' coming. This is the standard for Adventist marriages today. What the Whites and Paul said ultimately goes back to Jesus Himself. His words are true not only for those living in the first century but for us today, who are nearer Christ's coming than any previous generation. To each of us comes Jesus' challenge: "Seek ye first the kingdom of God, and his righteousness" (Matt. 6:33, KJV).

Use of my freedom, made possible by the blood of Christ,
must never be at the cost of someone else's well being,
for whom Christ also died.

Chapter 8

1 Corinthians 8:1–11:1

WHEN RIGHTS
EQUAL WRONGS

The real issue

"Free at last, free at last, thank God Almighty I'm free at last." The elite Corinthians would have endorsed this sentiment so powerfully delivered by the late Martin Luther King, Jr. Freedom to be and do is a marvelous gift from God. Every believer is meant to experience it. But, as with every other gift of the Christian life, it can be abused. Freedom from bondage may lead others into bondage when it is not tempered with love and concern for them. Christ has made us free (Gal. 5:1), but use of my freedom, made possible by the blood of Christ, must never be at the cost of someone else's well being, for whom Christ also died.

This issue comes to the fore in 1 Corinthians 8 where Paul deals with the question of eating meat offered to idols, another hot topic in the Corinthians' letter to Paul (7:1). The fact is that almost all meat eaten in Corinth would have been part of sacrifices to pagan gods. A portion of the meat of the sacrificial animal would have been burned on the temple altar, another part eaten by the priests in the temple services, and what remained sold in the public marketplace. This meat was rather expensive, and could be purchased regularly only by the more well-to-do. However, among the poor, who could not afford to buy it (their diets relying on grains and cereals, fruits and vegetables, along with some fish), the infrequent occasions when they could eat meat would be in the temple as part of feasts dedicated to honoring a god or at home as the result of a well-to-do person's gift in honor of a god. Temples at that time functioned not only as places of worship but as restaurants, serving their clients at banquets, club meetings, weddings, parties, and the like. Here sacrificial meat would be served.

Gentiles converted to Christianity naturally had questions about eating meat offered to pagan gods. Was this meat disqualified from the start because of its association with pagan worship and divinities? Could it be purchased and eaten in one's own home or in a friend's home? Would it be wrong to attend social gatherings in the temple and eat meat there?

These questions may sound remote and irrelevant to us. What could such concerns possibly have to do with us today? Everything! No, not the practice of eating idol meat as such, but the principles which undergird Paul's discussion of the question. These principles ultimately have to do not with meat, sacrifice, or idols, but with how one is to caringly relate to fellow members of the body of Christ. If a person has been given enlightenment and freedom in Christ, how does this affect relationships with those who may not have the same enlightenment, who may be what Paul calls the "weak" members of the church? They felt less free, more scrupulous, and had more sensitive consciences than their strong or liberal counterparts. Do those who have found knowledge and the freedom it inspires have any responsibility to their less mature brothers and sisters, or should they just do their own thing and forget the sensitivities of the weak and the impact of their deeds upon them?

When it comes down to it, the question is really about love. This is the note Paul strikes in 8:1. After quoting the Corinthian slogan "All of us possess knowledge," he says, "Knowledge puffs up, but love builds up." Knowledge may make us feel or look big, but it is only love, acting to support and strengthen others, which counts.

The slogan "All of us possess knowledge" may sound universalistic, but it was actually exclusivistic for, according to 8:7, not everyone had such knowledge. A certain group claimed special wisdom and the right to act entirely in accord with its knowledge regardless of how that affected others.

As we noticed in verses 4-6, it was the knowledge of God that certain of the Corinthians claimed. What they said about God was absolutely true: There was only one God, and the so-called gods thought to be behind the idols didn't really exist; so the eating of sacrificial meat was a matter of no consequence. Paul concurred with this when he confessed that there is only one God, the Father, from and for whom all things exist, and one Lord Jesus through whom all things exist (8:6). A wonderful truth, but one which does not qualify the person confessing it to claim that he knows as he ought to know (8:2). For example, the demons know the supreme truth, that there is only one God, but this is not saving knowledge, for it begets in them only shuddering fear rather than reverential love (James 2:19). First Corinthians 8:3 shows that what is needed is not mere knowledge about God but a love relationship with God which is a response to God's knowing us, that is, coming to us and drawing us into his fellowship (compare Gal. 4:9). The word "know" in the Bible often refers to an intimate relationship, but this is possible only because God makes the first move. "You did not choose me, but I chose you" (John 15:16). "We love because he first loved us" (1 John 4:19). Really knowing God in response to His finding us is the springboard not only to a relationship of love with God but to a caring, loving relationship with people. This is the true knowledge Paul taught in 1 Corinthians 8-10 and is why Jesus couples love for God with love for a neighbor (Mark 12:29-31; 1 John 4:20, 21).

Eating in an idol temple (8:7-13)

Though Paul would agree that the knowledge of one God permits one to eat idol meat (a position contrary to that of the weak), he disagrees that this allows one to eat sacrificial meat in the temple (contrary to the strong). He argues that among the Corinthian believers some do not have a sure knowledge of the one God. These are probably recent converts who are so accustomed to eating meat offered to a god that they cannot shake the feeling that there really is a god behind the idol. If they were influenced to go contrary to their true feelings and eat, their tender, new Christian consciences would be defiled

(8:7). What could lead them to go contrary to their conscience? The argument and practice of the strong. The strong argued—and Paul would undoubtedly agree in principle—that eating sacrificial food is inconsequential: "Food will not bring us close to God. We are not worse off if we do not eat, and no better off if we do" (8:8). The strong put this argument into practice by entering the temple of an idol and eating the meat offered there. Paul strenuously opposed this. The strong would not have a problem with such eating, but what about the weak? The acknowledged liberty of the strong must not become a stumbling block for the weak (8:9). And this could happen, for if the weak see the person of knowledge reclining at a meal in an idol temple, they might be encouraged to follow suit (8:10). The weak perform the same action, but they do not have the same inner security as the strong. They eat, but their conscience begins to make them feel guilty. Indeed, by acting contrary to their sense of right and wrong, no matter whether or not their conscience is fully enlightened, they actually sin against Christ. That is why Paul says that their conscience is defiled (8:7) and wounded (8:12), and they fall (8:13) and are destroyed (8:11). At whatever stage a Christian is, inner convictions concerning what is right must never be violated. The thing eaten or done may be innocent of itself, but if it is a violation of one's faith or conscience toward Christ it is sin, as also taught in Romans 14:23.

This reveals that sin is not only a deed but an attitude of disregard for one's own conviction about God's will. But sin is more than this. The weak sin by going contrary to their sense of God's will, but the strong sin by violating the bonds of relationship in the body of Christ. What of itself may be morally neutral may become inherently sinful when others are injured by what we do. Morality is not in things, but in relationships with others. It was the strong's irresponsible and flagrant use of their freedom that encouraged the weak to flout their conscience (8:10).

The problem with the strong in Corinth was that they forgot the very heart of the gospel: the self-giving love of Christ. And they forgot the gospel definition of our brothers and sisters in Christ: "believers for whom Christ died" (8:11; Rom. 14:15). In this light we must ask ourselves: How can I hurt one whom Christ died to heal? Is my personal freedom so valuable that its exercise is more important than the value God sets on others and the salvation Christ died to provide for them? Further, am I truly free if I have to do something just because my mind approves it, regardless of others? Christ's freedom was exhibited in His self-emptying (Phil. 2:6-8) and self-giving (Gal. 2:20). Paradoxically, am I not a slave to my freedom if I *must* act only in my own interests? The truly free are those who can freely give up their freedom for the sake of others, as Jesus did.

To think only of self and not of service is to sin against Christ (1 Cor. 8:12), who taught that what we do to others we do to Him (Matt. 15:40). Paul's attitude should be ours: "If food is a cause of their falling, I will never eat meat, so that I may not cause one of them to fall" (1 Cor. 8:13).

Paul had other grounds for saying believers should avoid eating in the dining halls of pagan temples. The pagan gods did not really exist, but evil powers did, and it is to them that the sacrifices were made (10:20). His conclusion is: "I do not want you to be partners with demons," for "You cannot partake of the table of the Lord (the Lord's Supper) and the table of demons" (10:21). Christians should stay out of any place and refuse any activity other than that which is dedicated to the Lord Jesus Christ and sanctified by His presence.

Eating in a private home (10:23-30)

In this passage Paul reiterates two principles which are fundamental to Christians' relationships with others. The first is that not all things which are lawful benefit the community. The question, especially relevant today, not only in ethics but also in politics and economics, is not whether something is legal, but whether it is right and good. Loopholes can be found in law, but not in a committed relationship of love. The second principle is that we are not to focus on our own good or advantage, but on that of the other person (10:24).

How unlike the world's standard this is. Ayn Rand in her book, *The Virtue of Selfishness*, and Robert Ringer, on a more popular level, in his *Winning Through Intimidation* (on bestseller lists for a long time), give voice to the world's view. Rand calls altruism (unselfishness) and giving one's self for others, especially strangers, completely irrational. To do such devalues self. The good of the self stands at the center of one's earthly universe, and the pleasure principle helps determine whether self is being served. Robert Ringer proposes what he calls the thirty-year theory. He suggests that in general we have about thirty years to live. What shall we do with our time? Life is like a poker game, in which we have only so many chips. The object of this life's game is to keep all of our own chips and get all the chips we can from others. No sticking our heads in the would-be sands of eternal life, declares Ringer. When this life is over we will not want to have missed any opportunities to get all we could for ourselves as quickly as possible. And how do we do this? By learning to exercise the power of intimidation over others!

Nothing could be further from the teaching and example of Christ (Eph. 4:20). From Him we learn that the essence of the Christian life is not intimidation of others, but imitation of Him who became a servant, willing even to give His life on a cross that salvation might come to full fruitage in us (Phil. 2:5-13).

With regard to eating, Paul advises that the principle of seeking the good of others be carried out in this way. Eat whatever is sold in the market without qualms of conscience, for the earth and everything in it belongs to the Lord (10:25, 26). One may therefore eat sacrificial meat at home or in the homes of unbelievers. No questions on the ground of conscience need be raised. But if a weaker brother or sister at the meal informs you that the meat has been sacrificed, then it should not be eaten for the sake of the sensitive conscience of that person (10:27, 28). A significant reason is then given why one should abstain in such a situation (10:29, 30), though the words of the text, isolated from the context, have been misinterpreted to mean that a person should be able to eat notwithstanding another's conscience. Paul reasons that the strong should refrain from eating so that their liberty will be protected from falling under the judgment of someone's weaker conscience. By desisting they will avoid being denounced over that for which they give thanks. Paul's argument here finds a clarifying parallel in Romans 14:15, 16: "If your brother or sister is being injured by what you eat, you are no longer walking in love . . . so do not let your good be spoken of as evil."

Imitators of Paul (11:1; 9:1-23)

Paul calls upon us in whatever we do, to do it for the glory of God without giving offense to anyone so that, by focusing on their advantage instead of our own, they may be saved (10:31, 32). The salvation of others is the bottom line and the supreme governing principle of Christian life. Because Paul both taught and exemplified this principle, he was able to say: "Be imitators of me as I am of Christ" (11:1). Christ is the ultimate illustration, but His servants are to be illustrations as well.

The non-exercise of one's own freedom and rights for the sake of the greater good of others is represented by Paul's apostolic life as recounted in 1 Corinthians 9. He contends that gospel workers have the right to material support from those who benefit from their ministry (9:1-14) but that he never sought this for himself (9:15-18). As in the previous argument, individuals may have rights they do not utilize so that larger ends may be achieved. The larger end Paul seeks to achieve is the announcement of God's free grace in Christ free of charge (19:15-18). In this way, his ministry would be a living representation of the message he preached. No wonder he could admonish, "Be imitators of me as I am of Christ" (11:1). Paul lived the truth he taught.

He did this particularly by being a servant to all—to Jews (those under Jewish law) and to Gentiles (those outside Jewish law). Most strikingly, he identified himself with those who were thought of as the weak, that he, unlike the strong, whose libertarian actions could destroy the weak, might save them for Christ. Indeed he became all things to all people—the incarnation principle—that he might by all means save some (9:22).

Freedom from evil (9:24–10:13)

Paul considered himself an example of true freedom. This freedom is not only freedom for salvation and service, but freedom from sin, without which real service for Christ is not possible. No one can serve two masters, Paul told the Romans (Rom. 6:16). But before Paul warns the Corinthians of the pitfall of sin which their false sense of freedom begets, he focuses upon himself and the possibility of his own spiritual demise. He still operates in terms of a model. As such he embodies not only the way of servanthood and salvation, but the way by which God's certain salvation could be lost. This may sound contradictory, but it is not. No one need be lost (10:12), but one could be lost if the proper acknowledgment of sin's reality and allurements is not made and appropriate discipline not exercised.

In 9:24-27 Paul uses the training and racing regimen of Greek athletes to teach that the "once saved, always saved" position is not tenable. To make it to the finish line of salvation, one must keep his eye on the goal line and winning the prize, and must exercise self-control in everything and strict discipline over his body. No "all things are lawful" here. An athlete cannot do just anything he wants. Not everything is beneficial; not all builds up. As to self-control and tough discipline, Paul says he does these very things with his bodily appetites, for having proclaimed the reality of salvation to others, he does not want to tragically end up disqualified himself.

The Corinthians needed to take this striking warning to heart. If their spiritual father could lose the race, so could they. They should not view their conversion to Christ, with the freedom it brought, as the achievement of an unalterable state of security that required no effort or vigilance. Rather, the redemptive freedom they experienced was an opportunity for growth in Christ—they had not yet arrived at the goal line, as they thought—which could be lost through neglect or abuse. The reason Paul talks about agonizingly exercising self-control (9:25, the Greek has the word *agonizo* in it) and of pummeling and restraining his body (9:27) is because of the Corinthian belief that what happened in the body had no consequence for the spiritual person within. Not so, says Paul. The bodily appetites, which may incline one to sin, must be held in subjection. The body matters.

In order to further counteract Corinthian presumptions about salvation as a kind of automatic reality with no connection to morality, in 10:1-12 Paul switches from his own life to Israel's history. Scripture contains no stronger rebuttal of the theology of "once saved, always saved, no matter what I do" than here.

Paul shows how Israel in the Exodus and wilderness experiences had the counterparts to the blessings of baptism and the Lord's Supper—rites deemed by the Corinthians as almost magical guarantees of salvation (baptism was even practiced for the dead to assure their salvation, 15:39). Israel had the equivalent of baptism into Christ, for it was baptized into Moses in the cloud and in the sea (10:1, 2). It experienced a foretaste of the Lord's Supper by partaking of the spiritual food (manna from heaven) and drinking the spiritual drink from Christ the Rock who followed them (10:3, 4). Notwithstanding their high privileges, most of Israel died in the wilderness because of God's displeasure with their rebellion against His will (10:5).

Paul sees a striking similarity between Israel's privileges and punishment and the privileges and possible doom of the Corinthians for the same kinds of reasons. If Christians desired evil as Israel did, punitive consequences must inevitably follow (10:6-11). The chief evils of Israel were idolatry and immorality. The Corinthians were in jeopardy for the same things. They were willing to involve themselves in eating food dedicated to heathen gods in the very temples of these gods, and they had partaken of sexual immorality as described in 1 Corinthians 5 and 6. Further, as Israel tested God by grumbling before Him (10:9, 10), so they had been testing Paul, God's apostle, with their complaints about him. The punch line is verse 12, where Paul admonishes that anyone who thinks that he stands (in the prideful belief of an unshakable salvation regardless of sin) should take heed lest he fall. Paul wanted to guard the Corinthians against a Christian edition of Israel's fall. The warning is dramatic but filled with God's saving grace, which comes to particular expression in verse 13, where Paul declares that despite the sternness of God's judgment against rebellion, there is no temptation which has come upon the Corinthians or anyone else for which God has not made a way of escape.

The antidote to the false gospels of "once saved, always saved, no matter what I may do," and "never quite saved no matter what Christ has done," is the true gospel of "continually assured of my salvation by continually remaining in union with Christ through faith."

The Lord's Supper is an acted parable. It proclaims to the world the significance of Jesus' death and how this death creates a new people who are awaiting His return.

Chapter 9

1 Corinthians 11

HONORING THE HEAD AND DISCERNING THE BODY

Freedom and order

As a herald of the gospel and church pastor, Paul had a twofold problem: how to make the new freedom of God's grace effective in the lives of believers, and how to protect this freedom from misuses which subvert the cause of Christ and give the gospel a bad name. In a word—how to balance grace and freedom with order and responsibility, a problem already seen in chapters 8-10.

In Galatians 3:28 Paul taught the fundamental gospel truth that in Christ the barriers between Jew and Gentile, slave and free, male and female had been broken down, and all had become one. This equality meant not merely that all, regardless of race, social status, and gender could equally come *to* Christ, but having come, that all must live equally *in* Christ. For example, Philemon was to receive the runaway Onesimus back, no longer as a slave, but as a beloved brother (Philemon 16).

The problem is how to make our oneness work on the practical level, where order must be maintained and cultural conventions not inimical to God respected. To unnecessarily flout culture, as with the issue of women and head coverings (11:2-16), would hinder the gospel. Christianity was revolutionary enough in its challenge to traditional gods and religion. It would not help the new movement to tear down the whole fabric of social custom and thus turn people away from Christ and the church.

81

Equality and interdependence

Two truths in 1 Corinthians 11 support the contention of Galatians 3:28 that male and female are one in Christ. The first is that women equally with men exercised leadership roles in public prayer and prophetic preaching (11:5). In dispensing gifts, the Spirit made no distinction between men and women in this regard. Joel 2:28, 29, cited in Acts 2:17, 18, says that in latter times God would pour out his Spirit on all flesh, and both males and females would receive the Spirit and prophesy.

The second truth is that "in the Lord woman is not independent of man or man independent of woman. For just as woman came from man, so man comes through woman" (11:11, 12). However, while man and woman are interdependent, they are both equally dependent on God (11:13). Subordination of female to male is not the issue here. Rather, Paul is arguing that when functioning as interdependent equals, women who participate publicly in worship should have a covering (probably a shawl), on their heads. Rejecting this cultural convention would disrupt divine worship and its purpose to glorify God.

Head coverings: Significance and reasons

When we interpret Scripture, we must distinguish between principles and policies, the timeless and the temporary, the universal and the local, Christ and culture. Clearly, the head coverings of Corinth were cultural, but that does not decrease their importance for that time, nor negate the necessity for us to find the principle involved for our time.

Why would head coverings for women be so significant in the Greco-Roman culture of that period? In general, the reasons embraced modesty and respectability, purity (for males in ancient times, the long hair of women was very seductive), the reservation of beauty for the husband alone, marital status, and gender identity. A woman praying or prophesying without a head covering in the ethnically and socially diverse church of Corinth might have been a source of offense to some, and a disturbing attraction to others. In that situation, that nothing detract from God's glory, women's heads needed to be covered. Uncovered women in worship might be associated with women with long, uncovered hair who worshiped in some of the pagan mystery religions. Frenzied, ecstatic behavior and long disheveled hair for both men and women were connected in some of these cults. In the cult of Isis, which had a major center in Corinth, women were admitted on the basis of complete equality with men.

It could well be that the uncovered women of Corinthian worship saw themselves as a kind of liberation movement, with long uncovered hair as a mark of their spiritual endowment, freedom, and identification with men. In harmony with the creation narratives of Genesis, Paul wanted to maintain the sexual *differentiation* God had created, not the sexual *identification* some in Corinth advocated with their belief that they were already living the transformed life of the resurrection where sexual distinctions no longer mattered. That may be why Paul, in 1 Corinthians 12:13 (unlike Gal. 3:28), did not include male and female in his list of classes of people who are one in Christ. To tell the Corinthians that males and females had become one might be misused to support their erroneous blurring of sexual differentiation.

Paul brings forth a number of arguments to support such head coverings. The first has to do with divine and human relationships (11:3-6). Paul declares that God is the head of Christ, Christ the head of man, and man the head of woman (11:3). If "head" means superiority over, as often suggested, the text is saying that God is superior to Christ and Christ is inferior and subordinate to God. These emphases do not fit the Corinthian context, for what would superiority and subordination mean in a context where both men and women participated in leading out in worship as interdependent equals?

However, the most frequent use of the term "head" is for that which in some way is the source of another. In terms of male and female this fits with verses 8 and 9 where, in dependence upon Genesis 2, woman was created from man as his companion. I would suggest that "head" is used in 1 Corinthians 11 to indicate the source through which authority is derived. The authority is actual but connected with another. If one's authority is derived, that person should not act in independence but in concert. A woman has authority—verse 10 literally says she has authority on her head—not independent of man but together with him. Certain Corinthian women, by not wearing head coverings, were signaling, in terms of the culture of the time, that they were independent of man in both their being and actions.

Thus, it is clear why Paul taught that in that day's culture women should be covered when actively involved in worship. It would be a sign of respect to the man, whose glory she was to be (11:7), not in the sense of being subordinate, but in that she would be his delight and honor, the one who makes his life and selfhood complete as bone of his bone and flesh of his flesh (Gen. 2:23) and his "equal" and "second self," as Ellen White put it in *Patriarchs and Prophets,* 46). The image of God would not be whole without both (Gen. 1:27).

However, what is not clear is why the concept of headship and derived authority meant for Paul that a woman should wear a covering so as to not shame her head, her husband, whereas the man should not wear a covering in relation to his head, Christ (11:4, 5). After all, Jewish men covered their heads with a shawl when praying to God and, among the Romans, both men and women wore a covering when bringing sacrifices to their gods or prophesying. The answer must lie in the peculiar situation in Corinth, where the biblical concept of the goodness of male and female differentiation was being lost.

Another question is why Paul supports his contention that men should not have a head covering in worship but women should by referring to Genesis 1:27 and 2:18-24 (1 Cor. 11:7-9). From Genesis 1 he deduces that man is the image and glory of God and from Genesis 2 that woman is the glory of man in that she was created from and for him. The difficulty is that in Genesis 1:26, 27 the word "man" does not refer to the male alone but to mankind composed of both male and female. Further, both are said to be in the image of God, the implication being that both together complete the image and manifest it in joint dominion over the earth. Surely, Genesis 2, in describing the woman created after the male as his "help" (a term often used in the Old Testament for God as the help of mankind), does not contradict the Genesis 1 picture of shared image and joint dominion. Perhaps we need to await Paul's explanation in the kingdom!

Verse 10 concludes Paul's argument thus far by saying: "For this reason a woman should have a symbol of authority on her head because of the angels." If the word "authority" is synonymous with covering, it must be stressing a particular function the covering has for the woman. Does this authority refer to that which a man exercises over her or which she exercises herself? It must be her authority, because the context is not discussing subjection, and the usage of the word authority by itself never refers to being under someone else's authority but to actively exercising one's own. To have authority is to be empowered to do something. How then can a woman's own authority be tied to being created from man? The answer seems simple enough. A woman's authority to pray and prophesy aloud is not to be disconnected from her relation to man. The covering is the cultural sign of that special relationship. With it on, she has the authority to exercise her spiritual giftedness by praying and prophesying equally with men. Her spiritual mandate to do so is related to the cultural mandate to be covered. Furthermore, in that culture, being covered in church would express propriety before the angels present in the worship service, with whom some of the Corinthians felt themselves to be joined in praising God (13:1).

Paul presents two other arguments to support women wearing head coverings, one from what is natural and the other from what is customary (11:13-16). As to the first, Paul teaches that when you take a general look at the order of things—there were many exceptions, of course—men have short hair and women have long. This suggests to Paul that as a man's hair is short, he should correspondingly not have a covering on his head, and as a woman's is long, she should have a covering corresponding to this. This argument may not have the same force today as in the first century, but it was important for Paul to pull out all the stops in attempting to correct a worship problem in first-century Corinth.

As to the argument from custom, he says that what he is

advocating here is in harmony with church practice everywhere, so, as the adage says, "When in Rome do as the Romans do!"

Modern relevance

What can we draw for our time from Paul's argument? First, it is important to be modest in dress for worship. Second, if the way we dress is discomforting to other worshipers, we should avoid it, for we are one body in Christ. Third, if our disregard of cultural conventions offends non-members and makes it difficult for them to come to Christ, we should think not merely of our own freedom but of their salvation. Fourth, in harmony with God's intention in creation, while working for unity, we must still preserve the differences between the sexes, and not do away with symbolic gender distinctions. Fifth, when culture conflicts with Christ, we must reject it, but when it may be used for Christ, we should respect it.

Lord's Supper or pagan banquet? (11:17-34)

In some cases it is important to follow cultural customs, but at other times not. According to Paul, the Lord's Supper was not the place for the Corinthians to carry on the practices of their pagan past. He is so unhappy over what they are doing that he cannot commend them at all, for when they get together to celebrate the Lord's meal, not the better but the worse takes place (11:17, 22).

Before describing the terrible wrong that was occurring, it will be helpful to see what the Lord's Supper means as Paul describes it in 1 Corinthians 10:16, 17 and 11:23-30. Three basic truths or realities are involved in eating the bread and drinking from the cup. The first is that we are sharing in the body and blood of Christ (10:16). Jesus stated: "This is my body that is for you" (11:24). He did not say "symbolizes" or "represents," but "is my body." "Sharing" and "is" refer to something more than a purely symbolic act. In order to avoid the over-sacramentalized Catholic view, Protestants have sometimes weakened the sense of these words. But in Paul's view, at the Supper we are not merely eating bread and drinking wine, but meaningfully participating in the body and blood of Christ. We become connected with the reality of His broken body and spilled blood as we eat.

Someone says: "But in 11:24, 25 the word 'remembrance' or 'memorial' is used. Does that not support a symbolic view, in that we are called to remember the body and blood as a past event?" The answer must be no, for the word "memorial" ("remembrance") has not merely a past but also a contemporary significance in the Bible. When God remembers the evil we have done, His divine judgment becomes a current reality to us, and when He remembers something good in our lives, His blessing comes to us. In other words, in the Bible remembering makes the past present, not only in the sense of mental recall, but also of experience in the present. Thus, as we remember Jesus' broken body and spilled blood, the saving power of these events nourishes our lives. We share in the presentness of God's salvation.

As a Catholic boy taking my first Holy Communion, I remember the impact of receiving the wafer upon my tongue, thinking that by the miracle of transubstantiation (the change of the bread's substance into the actual body of Christ), the living Christ was actually in my body. That was an imaginatively awesome experience. When I became a Seventh-day Adventist years later, my first Lord's Supper in my new church had a great impact on me. Adventists had taught me much about the symbolism of the Lord's Supper and, just as I had imagined the real presence of Christ on my tongue, I now imagined the historical reality of Jesus on Golgotha spilling His blood for me. I was totally touched; all the more so by the solemn and beautiful unity of all members of the congregation partaking of the emblems at the same time. It was a moving experience.

Some time later, as a student in an Adventist college, I decided to write a paper on the subject that had so intrigued me—the Lord's Supper. I was amazed at what I found in the chapter on the Supper in that classic study of Jesus, *The Desire of Ages*. Ellen White paints a balanced picture of our focus on the historical death and resurrection of Christ as redemptive events and the reality of Christ's presence during the Supper, but not in the elements, which remain only bread and wine. In entire harmony with biblical truth, she speaks much about the real presence of Christ in the chapter entitled "In Remembrance of Me!" She knew that memory and presence went together. Here are some of the data from that chapter. Several times Ellen White calls the Communion service a sacrament (653, 655, 659, 660). She did not accept the Catholic or Lutheran views of the real presence of Christ in the bread, but could use the word "sacrament" since it conveys the idea of a spiritual reality being mediated to us through a physical means. That is precisely what happens for us during the Supper. "Christ by the Holy Spirit is there to set the seal to His own ordinance. . . . For the repentant, brokenhearted one He is waiting. All things are ready for that soul's reception. . . . It is at these, His own appointments, that Christ meets His people, and energizes them by His presence. . . . Christ is there to minister to His children" (656). Then speaking of those who come to the Supper she says, "Now they come to meet with Christ. . . .in full consciousness of His presence, although unseen, they are to hear his words, 'Peace I leave with you'" (659). "As faith contemplates our Lord's great sacrifice, the soul assimilates the spiritual life of Christ. That soul will receive spiritual strength from every Communion. The service forms a living connection by which the believer is bound up with Christ" (661).

So, the first truth concerning the Supper is that, as we focus on Jesus' death for us, He is present spiritually to bless and strengthen us. The second concerns unity. Paul says that since we all partake of the same loaf, "we who are many are one body" (10:17). As the Lord's Supper forms a living connection between us and God (*The Desire of Ages*, p. 661), it also binds us who participate in it into one body. We are brothers and sisters, equal partners in God's salvation.

There is also a present and future dimension to the Lord's Supper: "For as often as you eat this bread and drink this cup, you proclaim the Lord's death until he comes" (11:26). The Lord's Supper is an acted parable. It proclaims to the world the significance of Jesus' death and how this death creates a new people who are awaiting His return. This proclamation of the Lord's death is the promise of, and prelude to, the future. The past of the death and resurrection of Jesus is present in the Supper, and the future of His coming again is already experienced by anticipation as we celebrate the meal with Jesus, our unseen Guest (see Rev. 3:20).

The perversion of the Supper

With these meanings inherent in the Lord's Supper, as taught by Paul, we can see why he would be devastated by the practices of certain of the Corinthians. Their holding to the cultural eating practices of their pagan lives was desecrating the Supper. "When you come together as a church, I hear that there are divisions among you" (11:18). The oneness of Christ's body, represented by the one loaf from which all partake, had been lost to view. How could church members partake of one Communion loaf and at the same time be divided into socially stratified groups? What a travesty of the meaning of unity!

In a phrase parallel to, and explanatory of, the significance of 11:18 concerning divisions, Paul says: "When you come together, it is not really to eat the Lord's supper, for when the time comes to eat, each of you goes ahead with your own supper, and one goes hungry and another becomes drunk" (11:20, 21). Apparently some Corinthians were not making a distinction between the pagan banquets and the Lord's Supper. In pagan banquets, the well-to-do ate the best food in the dining room of a home, which could accommodate only a small group. The larger number—poorer people—arrived later because they had to work late, and ate in the outer court from the scraps of food that were left or from meager, inferior fare prepared just for them. So the upper crust ate first, as they had in their pagan days, and the poor were left to wait in an inferior spot for inferior food, of which there was not always enough. Therefore, "one goes hungry," but at the same time, "another becomes drunk." Here the upper class, by the time the poor got a bit of food, were already getting drunk, as was customary for Greek banquets. Hunger for food is contrasted with excess of drink. What a picture!

Paul is livid with righteous indignation. He charges the "haves": If you are going to surfeit yourselves with food at the expense of others and wash it down with an extravagance of liquor, why don't you do it somewhere else than in a church gathering where by your actions you show contempt for the church of God and humiliate those who have nothing? (11:22).

The judgment of God

This is what Paul means by eating the bread and drinking the cup of the Lord in an unworthy manner (11:27). All who participate in divisions, selfishness, and disregard of the poor will be guilty of desecrating the body and blood of the Lord! (11:27). Christ died equally for all. Better examine yourselves then, admonishes Paul, for when you celebrate the Lord's Supper "without discerning the body," the presence of Christ whose body was broken for us that He might forge us into His body, the church, you bring the judgment of weakness, illness, and even death upon yourself (11:29, 30). Christ's death or your death are the only two choices, says Paul. So take your pick; what will your destiny be?

But the prospect of salvation reappears. The warning of judgment is "so that we might not be condemned along with the world" (11:32). So "when you come together to eat" (the agape feast with the Lord's Supper following), "wait for one another" (11:33). Concern for others, as God has been concerned for us, is the essence of the gospel.

Chapter 10

1 Corinthians 12

GOD'S NEW ARITHMETIC: MANY EQUALS ONE

Which is more important: unity in diversity or diversity in unity? Hard to tell, isn't it? Sometimes the accent needs to fall on the one and sometimes on the other. In 1 Corinthians 12 Paul stresses both and uses the human body to illustrate his teaching about the variety of spiritual gifts found in the one body of Christ. Both variety and oneness must be maintained together. If just variety is the focus, as among the Corinthians, chaos can result. If only oneness is stressed, the rich and diverse resources of God's grace may be missed. Sometimes only one gift is emphasized, such as tongues or prophecy, to the detriment of others. Often those acknowledged are the more spectacular in nature, such as healing or miracles, while less dramatic gifts such as teaching or helping are relegated to inferior positions. Using the analogy of the weaker or more hidden parts of the body, Paul argues against this (12:22-24). As there is great diversity in the same body, so also with gifts in the church. One equals many, and many equals one.

The true and the false (12:1-3)

Before pursuing his main argument about the gifts, Paul speaks about distinguishing between the genuine gifts of the Spirit and those manifestations that are not. Verse 1 really puts a damper on the spiritual haughtiness of some of the Corinthians. Does the word "spiritual" at the beginning mean "spiritual gifts" or "spiritual people"? Probably both, for spiritual persons exercise spiritual gifts. It undoubtedly came as somewhat of a put down to hear Paul say, "Now on this subject I do not want you to be ignorant." Ignorant? They felt so spiritually elevated that they would hardly have thought themselves ignorant!

Paul himself had affirmed their enrichment with spiritual gifts (1 Cor. 1:4-7). But it is one thing to have gifts and another to use them rightly. The Corinthians were using them to call attention to themselves rather than God. That is why Paul asked them: "What do you have that you did not receive? And if you received it why do you boast as if it were not a gift?" (4:7). Interestingly, Paul's favorite term for gifts is not *pneumatika*, used in 12:1, which probably is the Corinthian term emphasizing the source of the gift in the Spirit (*pneuma* means spirit). Rather, Paul prefers *charismata*, which means gifts of grace (*charis* denotes grace). He wanted them to remember that all they had was of grace and so to be thankful to God, not boastful of self.

They also made distinctions in the intrinsic value of the gifts—tongues was thought to be the greatest, even greater than prophecy—which automatically implied gradations in the importance of those exercising the gifts. This was another manifestation of the strong class consciousness in Corinth. Further, they so individualized the gifts, that they lost their purpose for building up the congregation rather than themselves. Everyone was practicing their particular gifts at the same time (14:26-33). The chaos that resulted chased mutual benefits away. What the Corinthians really needed, (though they thought they had it!) was the gift of wisdom to know how, when, and to what purpose to use the gifts, and the gift of love, without which the gifts had no center, and the community received no edification. To remedy the latter is why 1 Corinthians 13, the great love chapter, was written. When the lesson of love would be learned, wisdom for the proper use of the gifts would result.

Verses 2 and 3 are often glossed over by readers. They don't seem very clear, and their practical significance in the context is not readily apparent. However, what Paul says here is of outstanding importance. It is a test for the bottom line in the possession of the gifts. What are these gifts really doing and saying? What is the criterion for the genuine manifestation of the Spirit? To make his point Paul recalls the pagan days of the Corinthians (12:2). At that time "you were led astray to dumb idols, however you may have been moved" (RSV). The same basic Greek word (*ago*) is part of "led astray" and "moved." There is evidence that this verb could be used in reference to pagan ecstasy. Pagans, caught up in an ecstatic state, expressed what they thought to be inspired utterances as they worshiped before their "dumb idols."

Paul, setting the stage for his discussion of what the Corinthians believed to be their most exalted gift, tongues, (especially the tongues of angels, 13:1), wishes to make a contrast between their former pagan days, when the demons behind the dumb idols inspired their speech (10:20), and their present Christian experience when all so-called inspired utterances needed to be tested by their content and the benefits derived. An "inspired" state is not the final arbiter of truth. There are many spiritual experiences, but not all are from God. According to Paul, only what is confessed about Jesus counts. Is our Lord promoted or demoted? Here is the test for all claims of being in the Spirit.

Paul uses a negative and then a positive illustration of what he means. First, "no one speaking by the Spirit of God ever says 'Let Jesus be cursed!' " (2:3). Did anyone ever actually say such a thing, or does Paul use it merely as a stunning contrast to the real confession which follows, "No one can say 'Jesus is Lord' except by the Holy Spirit"?

There were those in the first century who made a division between Jesus and Christ, regarding Jesus as only an earthly man and Christ as a purely spiritual being who could not be identified with the physical Jesus. We have evidence of this view in 1 John. Such a person, in order to give expression to a purely spiritual view of Christ, might have said, "Jesus be cursed." And since Jews, in dependence upon Deuteronomy 21:23, easily could think that the crucified Jesus was under the curse of God, Paul might well have heard such a statement. Whether the statement is hypothetical or actual, a derogatory

pronouncement about Jesus could never have its source in God's
Spirit who inspires the confession of Jesus as Lord (12:3; Rom.
10:9; Phil. 2:11). So we are called upon to test the spirits to see
whether Jesus is being magnified by word and deed. The
Corinthians may have promoted Him in word, but the self-
centered and disordered way they used their spiritual gifts de-
tracted from Him as Lord.

The variety of gifts of the triune God (12:4-11)

While it is the Spirit of God which is emphasized in
1 Corinthians 12 as the source of the gifts, the initial description of these origins includes the Father, Son, and Spirit. The
three members of the Godhead represent the reality of diversity within unity. Trinity, it should be noted, is a shortened
form of Triunity. God's arithmetic is different: Three equals one.
In the listing in 12:4-6 notice the three-fold repetition of the
identical words for plurality and unity regarding each member
of the Godhead.

Endowment	Author	Plurality	Unity
Gifts	Spirit	varieties	same
Services	Lord	varieties	same
activities	God	varieties	same

Manifestly, all these gifts are meant to work in concert. That
is why verse 7, summarizing and applying verses 4-6 says, "To
each is given the manifestation of the Spirit for the common
good." The singular word "manifestation" is a summary of the
plural "gifts," "services," and "activities." In this way plurality
and unity are once again underscored.

The beginning of verse 7 as well as its ending brings something new. It begins, "To each is given." No one has all the gifts,
or even necessarily more than one gift, but there is an allot-
ment "to each one individually just as the Spirit chooses" (12:11).
At the end of the chapter, Paul asks, in a sevenfold repetition
of the word "all," if all are apostles, prophets, teachers, miracle
workers, healers, tongues speakers, or tongues interpreters?
The answer is obviously No.

Since spiritual gifts come from God's Spirit alone, we should be humble, and because each of us has a gift, we should be grateful. We need not covet anyone else's gift because the bestowal of gifts is by God's determination. He has graced us and we should be satisfied. Since no one has all the gifts, the ending of verse 7 is necessary. We are not to exercise our individual gifts for our private good, but for the common good. Unfortunately, we are often preoccupied with what we do not have, rather than what we do. Jealousy robs us of using our God-given gifts for the common good. As the old adage says, we are to be "one for all and all for one."

For purposes of comparison we may note the three lists of gifts given in 1 Corinthians as well as two other New Testament lists.

1 Cor. 12:4-7	1 Cor. 12:8-11	1 Cor. 12:28-31	Rom. 12:6-8	Eph. 4:11
gifts	wisdom	apostles	prophecy	apostles
services	knowledge	prophets	ministry	prophets
activities	faith	teachers	teaching	evangelists
manifestations	healing	deeds of power	exhortation	pastors
	miracles	healing	giving	teachers
	prophecy	assistance	leading	
	discernment of spirits	leadership	compassion	
	tongues	tongues		
	interpretation of tongues	interpretation of tongues		

Somewhere in these lists, which are more representative than exhaustive, our personal gift(s) may be located. Each of us should seek to discover our gifts, whether they are meant for a lifetime or a period of time, and make a concerted effort with God's help to use them in His service for the good of all. Our Spirit-chosen gifts may be a totally new creation for us, or may coincide with our God-given talents or abilities. When these talents are appointed by the Spirit to be used for the exaltation of Jesus and the good of His people, they become, at that point, spiritual gifts.

Perhaps our gifts have to do with assistance (1 Cor. 12:28) or compassion (Rom. 12:8). How marvelous! We may not be apostles or prophets, but think of the great benefit to the church when people help others with their problems or duties and show a compassionate attitude toward those struggling with sin or suffering.

As a new Adventist in college, I fondly and gratefully remember my first Bible teacher. Not only was I thrilled with the new Advent truths he taught me, which I eagerly devoured, but he set for me an example of being a helper and compassionate person. How well I recall this simple and unpretentious man standing in the hallway of the administration building every morning, greeting students and making them feel welcome! When I later became a faculty member there, he invited me to accompany him on voluntary rounds through the men's dormitories. He knocked on students' doors, entered their rooms, and sincerely asked how they were doing and if they had any special needs. Then he prayed for them. This humble teacher, I believe, will be surprised at the stars in his crown because of the many students he helped make it through college by bettering their spiritual and emotional welfare.

One body; many members

Ancient writers, even before the time of Paul, were fascinated by parallels between the structure of the human body and that of society, the "body-politic" in which each citizen had a role to play. Paul took this concept, poured the new wine of the gospel into it, and came up with a new creation in which the church, as the body of Christ, was compared with the human body. Each has many diverse members that contribute to the whole.

Though Paul uses the human body to illustrate his teaching, he means the word *body*, in reference to the church, to be understood quite literally. The church is a living, spiritual organism in which all members are bound together with each other in a shared life. That life is drawn from the risen Christ and is so identified with Him that when referring to the body of Christ in 12:12 Paul simply says "Christ" (though later he explicitly says: "You are the body of Christ," 12:27). Further, the life resident in the church through its identification with Christ expresses itself in love, as 1 Corinthians 13 makes clear.

Access to the body of Christ and the unity found in it is through the baptism of the Spirit. "For in the one Spirit we were all baptized into one body—Jews or Greeks, slaves or free—and we were all made to drink of one Spirit" (12:13). Entry into Christ is by baptism, according to Romans 6:3, and here entry into His body and the unity it comprises is by baptism as well. The positive significance of baptism should not be underplayed in an endeavor to counteract an exaggerated sacramentalism in some churches.

Baptism, as a time when faith comes to visible expression, is God's way of uniting us both to Christ and His people. It is like a marriage ceremony in which a new bond of togetherness is forged. Baptism is by water, though in 12:13 the accent is rightly upon the Holy Spirit, who makes water baptism a meaningful spiritual event rather than a purely physical event. The model for baptism is Jesus' own, when He, immersed in water, received the Spirit. Baptism and the reception of the Spirit are often coupled in the New Testament (Matt. 3:15; John 3:5; Acts 2:38; 3:19, 20; 19:5, 6; Titus 8:5). Some today teach that after water baptism we need to also receive Spirit baptism. This divides what God has joined together. We don't need a second baptism, but a closer attachment to, and walk in, the Spirit given us when we were first baptized. The electrical outlet is already wired and ready to supply power. We need only to put the plug of faith into it, and the power of the Spirit will be received.

In Paul's description of the various parts of the body, illustrating the variety of gifts in the church, a curious set of opposing statements is found. In the first, a foot, which does not feel secure in its place, since it is not a hand, says, "I do not belong to the body" (1 Cor. 12:15). Paul, of course, feels this is nonsensical, for if every organ of the body were the same, there wouldn't be a *body* (verse 19). The second statement made by one part of the body to another is, "I have no need of you" (verse 21). Paul replies to this by saying that all parts of the body are needed, especially the weaker or supposedly less honorable ones, to which God gives the greater honor! (verses 21-24).

These two statements reflect the stratification and dissension in the Corinthian church. Some felt inferior—undoubtedly under the influence of those with more striking gifts—and not a real part of the church. Others felt superior and independent from persons of supposed lesser gifts. Here we see the "have nots," who feel their gifts do not really count, and the "haves" agreeing with them. God's intention was to end this discord and inequality by having all members manifest the same quality of care for one another (verse 25). Since we have come to Christ as many members of His one body with diverse gifts, we are to remember our unity and the caring at its heart. "If one member suffers, all suffer together with it; if one member is honored, all rejoice together with it" (verse 26). Unity in suffering and joy—what a vision for those of us who belong to the same suffering Christ who rose again, and for our joy and good, gave gifts to us all (Eph. 4:10, 11).

Good, better, and best

The chapter closes with Paul reaffirming that all members of the church constitute the body of Christ—no upper or lower class citizens here—and this body is composed of a rich diversity of offices and gifts, rather than a uniformity. Then comes a final admonition and promise. The admonition to desire the higher gifts might sound at variance with Paul's previous argument that all gifts are good and for the common good. This seeming dissonance falls away when we realize that Paul is making a transition to his discussion in chapter 14 of how prophecy is more beneficial than tongues for the corporate body in worship, where intelligibility and edification are prime requirements. The Corinthians should desire the gifts that most effectively build up the congregation, rather than those that are more spectacular in nature.

But if all the gifts are good, though some better on a practical level for worship, Paul promises to show a way that is higher still. No member of the church possesses all the gifts, but all are to walk in the "more excellent way" of love.

According to Paul, perfection is not our achievement but God's gift from the future.

Chapter 11

1 Corinthians 13

LOVE BEATS ALL

The story of love

I was returning to my apartment from my day's classes at a graduate school in New York City. I followed the same route as always—up Broadway Avenue to 242nd street where I made a left turn. This particular day the light was red, so I was stopped. As I waited for the signal to turn green, I happened to look out my window toward the right, and there I saw a man—a dirty man—sitting in the street. His back was propped against a steel beam that supported the overhead tracks of the train system. His legs extended full length into the street; his arms were limp at his sides. His eyes were in a glassy stare, his nose running, his lips formed as if to cry out, but no sound came forth. I will never forget his face; it was the face of hopelessness, of lostness. The light turned green, and automatically it seemed, I made my left turn.

Granted, the man I saw was a very unattractive person, but unlike the Good Samaritan, I had done nothing to help him. I had not lifted a finger. *Why not?* I asked myself. But self-justifying thoughts ran through my mind. *Maybe you could not have helped him. Perhaps he was a mental case. If you had taken him home, he might have hurt you, or your wife or children. You might have gotten into something you wouldn't have been able to get yourself out of.* Rationalizations all, but the lost face kept intruding into my mind.

Another car was coming up the Broadway of our world. A

red light stopped the Driver. He looked out and saw you and me sitting dirty and lost in the street. Despite our unworthiness and unattractiveness, and the risk to Himself, He got out of His car, lifted us up, washed our wounds, and made something beautiful out of our lives—a new creation (2 Cor. 5:17).

The story of Jesus is the story of self-giving love, the love Ellen White describes as "the law of life for the universe" (*The Desire of Ages*, 21). The reality of this love completely changed the concept of love as represented in the Greek language of Paul's day.

Words for love

Among the Greeks there were a number of words for love. One was *erao*, used of that desirous love which seeks self-satisfaction in another person, particularly the fulfillment of sexual passion. *Phileo* represented the solicitous and warm love one has for a friend. *Agape*, only very rarely used outside the Bible, referred to the attraction or admiration one feels for a person of worth. Scripture made *agape* its chief word for love and completely transformed its meaning. It poured the new wine of the gospel into it and turned it on its head. *Agape* came to mean the principled and unconditional love that seeks to do all it can for another despite that person's unworthiness or ability to repay. It is based on the character of the lover rather than the character of the beloved. It is forgiveness of those who seem unforgivable, acceptance of the unacceptable, and love for the unlovable. It is the love seen in the Cross. "God proves his love for us in that while we were still sinners Christ died for us" (Rom. 5:8). In the light of this kind of love, when anyone says, "I love you," they should mean: "There is nothing I would not say, nothing I would not do to help you in your need. I am totally and ultimately concerned for you."

This was the kind of love Paul had in mind in 1 Corinthians 13 and what the factious, self-centered, and status-conscious Corinthians needed. It would be a rudder to steer them on the right course in the use of spiritual gifts. That is why Paul inserts this beautiful love poem into his argument. Love is not one of the spiritual gifts Paul discusses in chapters 12 and 14, though it is named first as a "fruit" of the Spirit in Galatians 5:22. Love is rather a way that transcends the spiritual gifts and yet transforms them to truly build up the congregation.

The greatness of love (verses 1-3)

Paul's first concern in 1 Corinthians 13 is to show the transcendent value of love. We may recall that when Jesus was asked by a Jewish expert in the law what the most important of the commandments was (the Jews had counted 613 commandments in the Law from Genesis through Deuteronomy), Jesus replied that loving God supremely and one's neighbor as oneself was the greatest of all. The lawyer agreed and added that love must then be greater than the greatest thing done in the holiest place of all—the offering of sacrifices of atonement in the temple (Mark 12:28-33). The lawyer had applied the supremacy of love to the most significant part of the religion of Israel. Each of us today should make the same type of application to what we consider important.

When Paul did that for the Corinthians, he showed that love was superior to the spiritual gifts they so prized and paraded. First, he said it was greater than the gift of tongues, not just earthly tongues but the tongues of angels as well. Here is the gift of communication, but of a special sort. First Corinthians 14 connects tongues with speaking to God (14:2) and with a special form of prayer, praise, and blessing (14:14-16). Mention of the angels gives the needed clue. Tongues was considered by the Corinthians to be a special kind of religious and spiritual experience, one in which the person felt not only in a spiritual state on earth, speaking to God in the tongues of earth, but he was, in a mystical way, transported to the realm of heaven to join the angel choirs as they worshiped God in the language of heaven.

This might sound strange to us today, but it was not at all strange to the Corinthians, who believed the resurrection of their inner self had already occurred. If they were already living the life of the resurrection—a reason why some in Corinth were for celibacy and against sex—it is not hard to see how some might feel they spoke the very language of heaven.

Thus, by "tongues speakers," Paul is making reference to persons who claimed a profound experience of God. His response to them is that no matter how intensely you feel yourself united to God, if you do not love God's children on earth, your tongues are no better than the noisy gongs and clanging cymbals used in the pagan worship services of that time. Thus, a deeply religious person without the love that is at the heart of God is no better than a pagan, for "God is love, and those who abide in love abide in God" (1 John 4:16).

What about the gift of prophecy? Wouldn't that make a person great? Not without love, says Paul. A prophet is not only one who predicts the future (the "pro" in prophet meaning "beforehand"), but especially one who speaks "forth" (another meaning of "pro") the word of God to convict people of their sins and cause them to recognize and return to God. This is what the Old Testament prophets did and how prophecy functioned in Corinth (13:24, 25). Paul's point then becomes clear: To function as a prophet and convict people of sin is of value only if you love the sinner. Of what value is censure without compassion, rebuke without tenderness? For Seventh-day Adventists, who prize the gift of prophecy, what Paul says here is of outstanding importance. The gift of prophecy has been manifested in our midst. It is a gift of love to be used in love. When employed only to condemn rather than to lovingly build up, it shatters God's purpose of love.

Knowledge has always been held in high esteem. Does it make a person great? Not without love. Knowledge can be very destructive without the rudder of love. We have so much technical knowledge today that we are able to destroy the world. What we need is love to foster and sustain life. Paul's estimate of knowledge is that it puffs up, but love builds up (8:1).

Miracle-working faith, which could even remove mountains, is another gift that might make a person look great. On television we hear again and again, "Expect a miracle." But what we need is not so much a miraculous faith, but a faith that works by love (Gal. 5:6), mends broken lives (Gal. 6:1), and removes the burdens from people's backs (Gal. 6:1, 2).

Giving away one's possessions would seem to be an act of

love, but this could be done to be praised by others (Matt. 6:1, 2), or perhaps to receive tax credits, and not really because of love. What people need is not just *what* we give but *who* we give—ourselves as those who love in Jesus' name.

Paul now brings into view a person who gives his body to be burned as a martyr. Wouldn't this be a great deed and an act of self-giving? Not unless there is a connection between this death and helping others. There is a story of a man who came from afar to Athens and burned himself alive after erecting a monument to himself with a boastful inscription announcing his immortality as a result of his self-immolation. Of what benefit was his death to anyone? If we were standing together in front of a burning house and I said, "I love you," and then ran into the house and perished in its flames, what would you think of me and the value of my deed? But if you were in the fire and I said, "I love you," and ran into the house to try to save you, at great risk to myself, that would really be love.

What God wants us to be is not primarily pious communicators, seers and judges, intellectuals, miracles workers, big givers, or martyrs, but lovers—those who have experienced God's love and share it with others.

The nature of love (13:4-7)

To describe what love is, Paul resorts to no lengthy philosophical discussion, but to a pithy description of the behavior of love. He lists fifteen verbs to show how love acts. The description begins with what love does, moves to what it doesn't do, and then returns again to what it does. The patience of love both begins and ends this description. Indeed, one of the cardinal characteristics of love is its staying power. It never ends (13:8).

The first two characteristics of love are two sides of a single coin. Patience, better translated as "long suffering" (KJV), is love's passive side, which has the capacity to withstand harm without giving way or retaliating. No one can say just how long a person should endure "the slings of outrageous fortune," but sufficiently to create a healing atmosphere, if at all possible. Our cue as to how to treat others is taken from God Himself, for He is "longsuffering to us, not willing that any should per-ish, but that all should come to repentance" (2 Pet. 3:9, KJV; compare Exod. 34:5, 6 and Ps. 103:8-14). Why is God patient with us? To create time for redemption to work. This should be our reason as well.

Flip the coin the other way and we have kindness or good-ness. Patience is passive, but kindness is active. Love never gives back in kind, but gives kindness instead. To get even with a hurtful person is to put ourselves on the same low level. As an action of love, kindness does not reject, ignore, or withdraw from another person, but does whatever it can to bless the life of that person regardless of who he or she is or has done. Jesus told us to "love your enemies, do good to those who hate you, bless those who curse you, pray for those who abuse you" (Luke 6:27, 28). And Paul said, bringing together both patience and kindness, "Do not be overcome by evil, but overcome evil with good" (Rom. 12:21). In abusive situations this may involve the goodness of "tough love," which takes a stand against abuse for the sake of helping both oneself and the abuser. Tough love, however, should always act in a kind way.

Jealousy and boastful pride are also two sides of a coin. Jeal-ousy, which keeps one purely on the level of the flesh (1 Cor. 3:3), does not provide others with space to exhibit their talents or grow, but wishes to confine them within the limits of one's own needs and insecurities. Jealousy is related to rivalry, com-petition, and greed, for it not only puts down the abilities and accomplishments of others, but inordinately desires for itself what others possess. True love, however, fosters others, not merely one's self. It sees itself as part of a community of shared richness, not in isolation.

Not only is love not jealous of what others have, but it does not go about parading what it has. It does not play the part of a balloon, swelling with ostentatious pride. This was a major Corinthian problem (4:6, 18, 19; 5:2; 8:1). It is obviously de-structive of the very meaning of community and the gratitude due God for the gifts He has given us (4:7). If love is not arro-gant, then, in a positive sense, it is humble—humble toward God and before others. It takes the attitude of our Lord, who emptied Himself (Phil. 2:7).

Further, love does not behave in an "unseemly" (KJV) manner. The word Paul uses here refers to that which is disgraceful, indecent, or shameful. It occurs in 1 Corinthians 11:22, describing the humiliation that the upper class put the poor through at the Lord's Supper. Thus, love never acts inappropriately toward others, in any way embarrassing them, disrespecting them, or treating them in a way that is rude or crude, gruff or tough. Love, in other words, has tender regard for the feelings of others. How many marriages and relationships could be saved if we all treated each other this way!

With the next characteristic we come into the holy of holies. "Love seeketh not her own" (KJV). The essence of the world's way is to seek its own rights and advantages, insisting on its own way without regard for others. Love can give up its rights when another person would be harmed by what we do. This is a repetition of 10:24, where Paul admonished: "Do not seek your own advantage, but that of the other." Paul took his own advice, not seeking his own advantage but that of the many, that they might be saved. In this he imitated Christ (10:33-11:1). When Christ went to the cross, He clearly was not seeking His rights (He did not think His equality with God had to be held on to, Phil. 2:6), but our salvation. When we act in this way, we are most truly acting like Jesus. Again, how many relationships could be saved if we were thinking about the good of others and not just our own selfish concerns!

The next characteristic is connected with the preceding. People get mad when they don't get their way, but since love does not seek its own, it has no reason for anger. The word Paul uses has been transliterated into English from the Greek as "paroxysm." It is much stronger than anger, and refers to flying into a rage or having a fit or temper tantrum. When one is consumed by wrath against another because that person seemingly interfered with his rights, he can be sure he is not walking the pathway of love. Hotheads do not belong on the trail leading to God's kingdom of peace. Only the peaceable travel there.

Again, we are in the holy of holies with the declaration that love thinks no evil, as the KJV says. Actually, while the word Paul uses here (*logizomai*) may mean "think," there is a better translation. Paul is not teaching that the loving person never has a wrong thought—though that is an ideal we hope to reach by God's grace. Rather, he is saying that love does not reckon or count up the wrongs of others against us. It does not play the part of an archaeologist, digging up the dirty past! *Logizomai* (reckon) is utilized by Paul in major passages to teach that God reckons or imputes His righteousness to us but does not count our sins against us (in Romans 4 frequently; also 2 Cor. 5:19). Love asks us to do for one another what God has done for us (see Col. 2:13). Not counting sins, then, means that we are challenged to forgive those who have hurt us, rather than keeping a scorecard of their wrongs and storing up resentment and bitterness against them. Jesus' prayer is to be ours, "Father forgive them, for they do not know what they are doing" (Luke 23:34).

As Paul winds up his list of love's attributes, he says it does not rejoice in wrongdoing but in the truth of right doing, and it bears, believes, hopes, and endures all things. By "believes and hopes all things," is Paul saying that love is gullible? I think not. He is teaching that love is optimistic. It believes that compassion is greater than cruelty, and love stronger than hate. Love can outlast anything (13:8). It looks forward to its final victory when all things animate and inanimate, from the smallest atom to the greatest world, will declare that God is love (*The Great Controversy*, 678).

The eternity of love (8-13)

As the character of God and the law of life for the universe, love will never pass away. It is the final truth. Tongues, present knowledge, and prophecy, however, will come to an end, for as helpful as these things have been, they are incomplete and imperfect. This was news to the Corinthians, for they believed tongues brought them into God's presence, and prophecy and knowledge to ultimate truth, exalting their possessor above others. "But when the perfect comes" is a correction of those who thought they were already perfect and had already arrived.

According to Paul, perfection is not our achievement but God's gift from the future. A realized eschatology (the belief that the kingdom had already come in their lives), such as the Corinthians held, could never be true. Right now "we see through a glass darkly" (KJV). "Glass" here refers to the mirrors that the Corinthians produced out of polished bronze that could never give a clear picture. The Greek word translated "darkly" is *ainigma*, from which we get the English word enigma. We see into the mirror of present reality as into an enigma, a puzzle, a riddle. Life just doesn't make sense at times. But in the future the puzzling distortions of this world will be gone, and we shall see face to face, with nothing between to cloud our vision of ultimate reality. The redeemed will see God's face (Rev. 22:4), and having grown from the childhood of this world to the maturity of the next, we will know Him with a fullness of understanding that corresponds to His already complete knowledge of us. This is the meaning of 13:12 rather than the otherwise true idea that we shall know each other in heaven. The one whom we have been needing and wanting to know is God. But until His glory is revealed to us we can rest in the confidence that He knows all about us and accepts us in His love.

Before Jesus returns, bringing with Him the perfection of the world beyond, there are three things that remain: faith, hope, and love, but the greatest of these is love. Why is love greater than faith and hope? First, because love is the basis for faith and hope. We have faith and hope because God has come to us in His love. Second, we will not need faith and hope in God's eternal world, for then we will walk by sight. Faith, not sight, is the present condition of things (2 Cor. 5:7). Of these three virtues only love will last throughout eternity. Lastly, faith and hope are human, not divine qualities. God is not believing and hoping against hope as we are (Rom. 4:18). Love is the one characteristic we share with God.

In the time remaining until Christ returns, let us trust in God and not sit in the seat of scoffers, hope in God and not stand in the place of cynics, and above all, love one another, as God has loved us.

Holiness is not rapture: it is an entire surrender of the will
to God . . . it is doing the will of our heavenly Father
(The Acts of the Apostles, 50).

Chapter 12

1 Corinthians 14

UNTANGLING TANGLED TONGUES

With love firmly in place as the indispensable foundation of the church's life, Paul turns to the function of Spirit-inspired speech. His concern is with tongues and prophecy. With love as the motivating force, manifestations of the Spirit appropriate to public worship are meant to build up the congregation (verses 4-5, 12, 17, 26), not divide it; to be intelligible, not unintelligible; and to be exercised in an atmosphere of order, not disorder. Intelligibility and order are meant to make building up possible.

The greatest gift for public worship

The principle of intelligibility is pursued in 14:1-15 in the context of a comparison between tongues and prophecy. When the criteria for proper worship are applied, prophecy emerges as supreme. Paul plainly says: "Strive for the spiritual gifts, and especially that you may prophesy" (14:1). As the content of the discussion makes certain, the principal reason why prophecy is better than tongues for worship is the innate nature of these gifts, not their misuse. Prophecy's precedence over tongues resides in the areas of function and intended audience.

Reasons for Paul's challenge to especially seek prophecy are given in the verses which follow. The first is that the gift of tongues is directed to God, not people. Tongues, therefore, has a basically vertical dimension. In speaking to God, says Paul, persons with this gift are declaring mysteries or secret things not open to others. That is why nobody understands them (14:2).

But prophecy is horizontal in nature. Unlike tongues, it intends to bring them upbuilding, encouragement, consolation (14:3); also reproof, accountability, and disclosure of the heart's secrets and God's presence (14:24-25). In 14:5 Paul draws a conclusion from verses 2-4 that brings us back to his emphasis on the superiority of prophecy in verse 1. He says his wish for the Corinthians to prophesy is stronger than his wish that they speak in tongues. For the building up of the church, which worship requires, "one who prophesies is greater than one who speaks in tongues, unless someone interprets" (14:5). The necessity of an interpreter is to explain the mysteries spoken (14:2). If the church is going to get any benefit, the secrets have to be revealed! No revelation, no edification!

In 14:1-5 Paul's emphasis has been on the superiority of prophecy. In 14:6-11 he places the accent on the inferiority of tongues. His thesis in this section is that only intelligible utterances strengthen the church, and he admonishes the church to strive for excellence in doing this (14:12). He begins by asking what benefit the church would get from his coming to them speaking in tongues—the Corinthians undoubtedly accused him of not doing this—if he did not bring some revelation, knowledge, prophecy, or teaching (14:6). None, of course! Each of these forms of instruction and edification speak directly to the congregation, but tongues do not (14:2).

Then Paul presents three analogies with which he compares tongues. Tongues are like flutes, harps, or bugles which, if they do not play distinct notes, will not help the audience to experience music, or soldiers to get ready for battle. The conclusion is that if unintelligible speech is uttered, the speaker will be speaking into the air, for no one will know what is said (14:9).

Paul also says tongues are like the "sounds" of languages (the Greek word literally means "sounds") that cannot be understood and hence leave everyone foreigners to each other (14:10-11). The conclusion is irresistible: tongues, by their very nature, are valueless for church worship.

In 14:13-25 Paul presents a second series of arguments for the inferiority of tongues. He begins with an exhortation that the tongues speaker pray for the power to interpret (14:13), which implies that the experience is not one of the mind. Prayer is not needed for what the mind knows and can state clearly. This is why Paul says in verse 14 that in the experience of tongues the spirit of the person is involved, but his mind is unfruitful, that is, dormant or unproductive. The *Seventh-day Adventist Bible Commentary* is accurate when it presents the possibility that the experience of tongues is not one of the conscious mind (6:789). Otherwise, the contrast in 14:14-16, 19, between what one does with his spirit (a reference to tongues) and his mind makes no sense. Some interpret "my mind is unfruitful" as meaning "other people's understanding of me is unfruitful." This cannot be, for the mind and the spirit are parallel here, and both are obviously faculties of the person who speaks. The spirit certainly does not refer to anything in the hearers. That mind is a reference to the speaker's own faculty is clear from verse 19, where the use of the mind is to instruct others.

In verses 14-17, tongues, as a function of the spirit of a person, are equated with praying, praising, blessing, or giving thanks to God. According to the passage, one can also do these things with the mind. This shows that tongues cannot be a mental experience. If they were, spirit (tongues) and mind could not be contrasted. Paul recommends that in church prayer and praise be carried on in the mind so that others, who would not understand tongues, will be able to say "Amen" and be built up (16-17). His conclusion is that though he himself possesses the gift of tongues, he would much rather speak a mere five words with his mind to instruct others than ten thousand words in a tongue! So much for the value of tongues for public worship!

Paul now clinches his argument that tongues are clearly inferior to prophecy. After appealing to maturity of thought (14:13)—another blow to the belief of some Corinthians that they had already arrived at total maturity—in 14:21 Paul quotes from Isaiah 28:11-12, which is part of a chapter on judgment against Israel. Here sinful Israel will not heed God and turn back to Him when it hears the unintelligible tongues of the Assyrians, who were God's agents of judgment. From this, Paul concludes that tongues are a sign for unbelievers and prophecy a sign for believers.

Some have interpreted "sign for unbelievers" as "sign for the conversion of unbelievers." This is the complete opposite of the meaning of both the Isaiah text, which leaves Israel unconverted after hearing the tongues, and Paul's description of what happens when outsiders or unbelievers enter the church and hear its members speaking either in tongues or in prophecy. When these non-members hear speaking in tongues, "will they not say that you are out of your mind?" (14:23). As Isaiah predicted, tongues only confirm unbelievers in their unbelieving ways. They see in them no sign of the presence of God. But when unbelievers witness the phenomenon of prophecy by church members, they are reproved by all and called to account (14:24). After the secrets of the unbeliever's heart are disclosed, that person will bow down before God and worship Him, declaring "God is really among you" (14:25). Prophecy, not tongues, converts unbelievers.

Thus, tongues are a negative sign for unbelievers—teaching them nothing—but prophecy is a positive sign for believers, teaching them what really moves unbelievers to God and gives deepest evidence of His presence.

Tongues: Foreign languages or emotive utterances?

It has been argued vigorously that an obscure text (supposedly 1 Corinthians 14) should be interpreted in the light of a clear text (Acts 2 and the tongues of Pentecost). This is incorrect on three counts. One, every text should be first understood in the light of its own context and content. Only then may it appropriately be compared with another text. Too often, in the interests of a contemporary need (to combat false theology or practice), or to preserve a previously held viewpoint, one text is wrongly forced into another. Second, God's word in 1 Corinthians 14 is clear, not obscure. First Corinthians was written before Acts, and was meant to be understood by itself. Third, the converting power of tongues in Acts 2, 10, and 19 is questionable. Another function is discernible.

Though tongues in 1 Corinthians 14 must be understood in

the setting of 1 Corinthians, I turn first to Acts, in deference to those who suggest this, to see what Acts says in its context. It does not really matter where one starts as long as the content of each passage is given its due weight. When that is done, it will be seen that tongues in Acts refers to foreign languages whereas in 1 Corinthians it does not.

The evidence of acts

The day of Pentecost, when the Spirit descended upon Jesus' disciples, was the birthday of the Church. Three thousand were converted to Christ on this day. How did it happen? The disciples of Jesus were assembled. The Holy Spirit descended from heaven like the rush of the wind, and tongues of fire distributed themselves over the disciples. Filled with the Spirit, they began to speak in other languages as the Holy Spirit gave them ability (Acts 2:4). As the disciples spoke, they were not moving through the crowd, but "were all together in one place" (2:1). The crowd, composed of Jews from every nation, moved to the disciples because they heard the sound of all of them speaking in the intelligible languages of their homelands (1:5-6, 8).

What were the disciples saying? According to 2:11, they were speaking about God's "great deeds" (literal translation of the Greek *megaleia*). In other words, they were extolling God for His mighty acts of salvation. This was a testimony and praise service, and it attracted a crowd.

What reaction did the crowd have? "All were amazed and perplexed, saying to one another, 'What does this mean?' But others sneered and said, 'They are filled with new wine' " (2:12, 13; see also 2:6, 7). Amazement, bewilderment, scoffing, and a charge of drunkenness—these were the crowd's reactions, not faith, repentance, and turning to Christ. Tongues converted no one on the day of Pentecost.

What did convert the people? It was the preaching of Peter in a language most everyone could understand. The text gives no indication that he used the gift of tongues in his speech about the fulfillment of prophecy in the life, death, and resurrection of Jesus. To the contrary, he was explaining the tongues phenomenon in view of the negative and puzzled reactions it caused.

He did so by making use of a common language, probably Greek, the *lingua franca* of the Greco-Roman empire, the language in which all the writings of the New Testament were composed, despite the variety of locations to which they were sent.

If the tongues phenomenon did not have the purpose of converting people, what purpose did it have? Jews came to believe that Pentecost, in addition to its original Old Testament significance, celebrated the giving of the law at Sinai in all the languages of earth. Now, as the church is born on Pentecost, the languages of earth are spoken by the disciples, indicating that the gospel is universal, and praise of God for His mighty deeds is to sound forth everywhere, in the speech of every nation.

We see this in the case of the Gentile Cornelius and his group in Acts 10. After Peter preached the gospel of the life, death, and resurrection of Jesus to them and they received the Holy Spirit as the emblem of their acceptance into the people of God, they broke out in tongues, "extolling" God (10:46). "Extolling" is the translation of *megalynonton*, a word related to the disciples' speaking the *megaleia* ("great deeds") of God in Acts 2:11. In other words, the converted spoke in tongues, not the evangelist Peter. Tongues were the response of praise for the gospel of God's mighty deeds in Jesus, not the cause of conversion. It is the same in Acts 19:5-7, where subsequent to baptism, the laying on of hands, and the reception of the Spirit, a group of twelve began to speak in tongues. Again the tongues were not an evangelistic tool but an evangelistic result.

Outside of these three passages, tongues play no part in the extensive evangelism depicted in Acts. In fact, in the New Testament, tongues never are spoken of as converting anyone. In Mark 16:17 speaking in tongues is not pictured as leading to belief, but as accompanying those who already believed.

Ellen White and tongues

Ellen White, in dealing with the tongues of Pentecost and Ephesus, does mention that this gift enabled the apostles and the converted to labor as missionaries (see *The Acts of the Apostles*, 39, 40; *Testimonies for the Church*, 5:391). At the same time, she stated that "the world will not be converted by the gift of tongues, or by the working of miracles, but by preaching Christ crucified" (*Testimonies to Ministers*, 424). Further, in describing the time of Jesus as the "fullness of time," when conditions would make it easier for the gospel to be spread, she states the fact that along with the nations being united under one government, the Greek language "was widely spoken, and was everywhere recognized as the language of literature" (*The Desire of Ages*, 32). She adds that "for hundreds of years the Scriptures had been translated into the Greek language, then widely spoken throughout the Roman Empire" (*The Desire of Ages*, 33). Thus, much of the evangelism of Paul's day could be carried on in Greek. Generally, tongues would not be needed.

The evidence of 1 Corinthians 14

We have seen from Scripture, looked at by itself as the inspired Word of God, that tongues are not presented as an evangelistic tool. And we have noted that in Acts tongues are connected with praising God for His marvelous deeds. It remains to show that 1 Corinthians 14 does not identify tongues as foreign languages for evangelism.

One would have to bring the foreign language view to the chapter to be able to find it there. Surely, if the gift of tongues was evangelistic, we would find some hint of it. What we do find are the following: (1) In listing a number of characteristics of tongues, Paul does not call them abuses of the gift, but assumes them as the content of the gift. These include the fact that tongues are addressed to God, edify the speaker, not others, and are utterances of secret things (1 Cor. 14:2-4). If these were abuses, Paul could have demanded that tongues be used rightly, as he did in connection with disorder (14:27). (2) Paul says the tongues speakers should pray for the power to interpret (14:13). Why, if this is a foreign language? All the speakers had to do was use the Greek language in a Greek church. In fact the whole notion of an interpreter, mentioned a number of times in the chapter, is strange if foreign languages for evangelism were meant. The purpose of such a gift would have been to make an interpreter unnecessary. Furthermore, why would

God endow someone to interpret the misuse of a foreign language gift? Is God an accomplice to a gift's perversion? The gifts are given as the Spirit chooses (12:11). Why would the Spirit choose to pander in this way? (3) Since tongues are compared with unintelligible foreign languages (14:10, 11), how can they be these languages? You don't compare a thing with itself. It makes no sense to say, "Foreign languages are like foreign languages!" Besides, tongues are compared with musical instruments as well (2:7, 8). Foreign languages are not the issue here. (4) How would the gift of foreign languages—a rational experience—make the mind unfruitful or dormant (14:14)? This does not make sense. (5) Foreign languages for evangelism would be meant for the conversion of unbelievers, but unbelievers are not helped by tongues at all, but call the speakers "out of your mind" (14:23). Unbelievers are converted by prophecy (14:24, 25). (6) Why does Paul urge tongues speakers to be silent if there is no interpreter, and speak only to themselves and God? (14:28). (7) If Paul is considering a false use of foreign languages, how could he say, "Do not forbid speaking in tongues"? (14:39). And if the proper use of languages is in view, why would he not say, as he does of prophecy in the same verse, "Be eager to use tongues"?

Conclusion

Our conclusion is that in Corinth tongues operated as an emotive rather than rational gift. It was a private gift, especially suited to the religious temperament of Greek worshipers at the time, and having to do with a special form of prayer and praise to God (14:15-17). Because it was private, edifying only the tongues speaker, Paul sought to excise it from public worship unless there was an interpreter, and no more than two or three spoke (14:27, 28). Thus, Paul put a premium on the orderly in public worship and sought to contain, though not exclude the emotional, when it could be edifying to all.

Today, charismatic churches to a significant extent have gone contrary to Paul. What he puts in last position in the lists of gifts in 1 Corinthians 12—last because they fundamentally are not of benefit for others—they put first, and some almost insist that all speak in tongues, whereas Paul emphasizes that not all are gifted in this or that way (12:29, 30).

In the spirit of Paul in 1 Corinthians 14, and with a concern that emotion in religion, while necessary, not get out of hand, a balancing truth for Adventists is best expressed by Ellen White:

> It is not a conclusive evidence that a man is a Christian because he manifests spiritual ecstasy under extraordinary circumstances. Holiness is not rapture: it is an entire surrender of the will to God; it is living by every word that proceeds from the mouth of God; it is doing the will of our heavenly Father; it is trusting God in trial, in darkness as well as in the light; it is walking by faith and not by sight; it is relying on God with unquestioning confidence, and resting in His love (*The Acts of the Apostles*, 51).

*The gospel is not good advice, but good news
because it tells the story of what happened
to Jesus and what therefore happened for us.*

Chapter 13

1 Corinthians 15

RESURRECTING THE RESURRECTION

Longing for the resurrection

When you have lost someone you really love, the resurrection becomes a key reality. Everyone has had, or will have, such losses. I have had my share. I loved my father. When he returned to his homeland, Croatia—his first visit after coming to America at about the age of ten—he died of a massive heart attack. My heart broke, but I am looking forward to the day of resurrection when I and my father, who was influenced toward the Advent faith as a result of the love of Seventh-day Adventists in Croatia, will meet again.

She was a wonderful person, my first wife and the mother of my children, but cancer took her life away. Her love for Jesus was strong, however, and my daughters and I fully believe our living Lord will restore her to life again when the resurrection comes. It must come.

My wife of today lost her first husband to a massive heart attack and, a few days after she and I were married, her only two children died in a horrible car crash. I remember sitting with her in the cemetery in front of the two coffins of her children soon to be buried. The minister quoted the words: " 'I am the resurrection and the life. Those who believe in me, even though they die, will live' " (John 11:25). I heard my wife say, "Yes!" She and I with other family members, painfully, agonizingly long for the resurrection when we will be with our loved ones again. That time cannot arrive too soon.

119

Without the truth of the resurrection to come, where would we be? Our hope rests upon its certainty, which is grounded in the resurrection of Jesus.

Denial of the resurrection

It comes as a shock to find that members of the Corinthian congregation denied the resurrection of the dead (1 Cor. 15:12). Their belief in a present spiritual resurrection of the living made a resurrection of the dead nonsensical and superfluous. Because their inner selves had become spiritually transformed by the Spirit's power, they had all they wanted, and were rich and reigning as kings (4:8). And since in Greek thought the body was transient while the spirit within man was eternal, the resurrection of the body was ridiculous. Their mocking questions were: " 'How are the dead raised? With what kind of body do they come?' " (15:35). In other words, how is it possible to conceive of a resurrection at all? Can there be a body out of a decomposed rubbish heap?

They must have thought that resurrection meant the resuscitation of the old body. But as Celsus, the third-century pagan critic of Christianity said, that would be "the hope of worms, for what soul of a man would any longer wish for a body that had rotted?" When Paul spoke to the Athenian philosophers about the resurrection, some scoffed while others deferred discussion (Acts 17:32). In general for the Greeks, getting rid of the body so the spirit could be free to wing its way back to the heavenly realm was salvation—they saw no need for a resurrection of the body. Socrates could drink the hemlock—the method of his execution—with complete serenity because he believed his spirit would be freed from his body. The Greeks compared the body to a tomb or to a corpse to which the soul was shackled.

The New Testament gives evidence that some Christians believed in an eschatology of the present rather than the future. In 2 Timothy 2:17, 18 Paul refers to "Hymenaeus and Philetus, who have swerved from the truth by claiming that the resurrection has already taken place. They are upsetting the faith of some." In 2 Thessalonians 2:2 we read about those who said that the day of the Lord was already here.

The Corinthian deniers were not saying there is no resurrection at all but that there is no resurrection of the dead, meaning no *future* resurrection of the *body*. Death dissolves the body, so how could there possibly be a bodily resurrection in the future?

They obviously were reasoning from this world to the next and placing limitations on the future by reason of the limitations of the present. In this regard they were similar to the Sadducees who, as unbelievers in the resurrection, came to Jesus with a question designed to show its absurdity (Mark 12:18-27). Suppose, they said, that a woman had seven husbands who died. In the resurrection, whose wife would she be? The question was meant to show the irrationality of the idea of resurrection life. It would pose so many problems that it was absurd to believe it. Jesus responded that they were guilty of a twofold error: not knowing the Scriptures—they accepted only Genesis through Deuteronomy as authoritative, and no resurrection is mentioned there—and not knowing the power of God, which can make all things new. Their problem was like that of the Corinthians: judging future possibilities based on present realities. Jesus' answer, as also Paul's, was that the deniers of the resurrection did not know the God of creation. As Creator, God is not limited by conditions in this world. We are limited in that we cannot see past this world, but that does not mean that there is not something new to come.

Arguments for the resurrection

How would you go about convincing the Corinthian skeptics that there would be a resurrection of the dead? Here is how Paul did it. His argument began not with philosophical speculation (which would have suited the Corinthians just fine) but with the reality of Christ's resurrection, which Paul had proclaimed to them, to which they had agreed, and by which they had become Christians. His message of the risen Christ was the means of their salvation, *but only if they held firmly to it* (1 Cor. 15:1, 2).

The original gospel message that Paul had received and

had handed on to them is contained in the earliest Christian confession of faith we possess (15:3-5). It goes like this:

> Christ died for our sins according to the Scriptures
> and was buried.
> He rose the third day according to the Scriptures
> and was seen.

Here is the gospel in a nutshell. In harmony with Scripture, Christ died as an atoning sacrifice and was buried as proof of His death. He rose the third day and appeared as proof of His resurrection. The gospel is not good advice, but good news because it tells the story of what happened to Jesus and what, therefore, happened for us. The resurrection of Jesus is central to that story, and it is not a cunningly devised fable, for He was seen by many in His risen state: Cephas, the twelve, five hundred plus, James, all the apostles (again, or another group), and last of all to Paul (15:4-8).

Since the Corinthians had believed in the proclamation of Jesus' resurrection (15:11), how could they deny the resurrection of others? (15:12). They must have conceived of Jesus' resurrection as a unique spiritual event that was presently duplicated in their lives through their reception of the Spirit, as evidenced by the spiritual gifts they had been granted. The completeness of their transformation was demonstrated in particular through the gift of tongues by which they believed they spoke the angelic language of the heavenly world, the life of which they had now attained.

Over against this Paul taught that there is a direct corollary between the resurrection of Christ and the future resurrection of the dead. Deny that the dead rise, and you must also deny that Christ rose. The results of this would be devastating. Without a risen Christ, Paul's gospel proclamation and their faith in it are empty of meaning, the apostles turn out to be misrepresenting God, faith becomes futility, believers are yet in their sins, the dead have perished forever, and Christians become the most pathetic people on earth, for their hope extends no farther than this world—and that isn't hope at all (15:12-19).

However, if Christ has been raised, a totally different set of consequences follow. Through His resurrection He becomes the first fruits of those who have died, that is, the pledge of a harvest of resurrected ones to come. The principle of solidarity is at work here. We are not solitary individuals, but a body bound together with Christ as our head. What happens to the head happens to us. Thus, as "in Adam all die, so also in Christ *shall all* be made alive. But each in his own order: Christ the first fruits, then at his coming those who belong to Christ" (15:22, 23, RSV).

The Corinthians had it wrong. Only Christ had been raised, not themselves. There is a resurrection of "those who belong to Christ," but not yet, only at His coming. Paul points them to a future resurrection and establishment of the kingdom, as opposed to their idea that Christ had already accomplished this in them. He explicitly declares, "Then comes the end," (15:24) referring to a time subsequent to the coming of Christ mentioned in verse 23.

Not only does Jesus' resurrection portend a great harvest to follow, but it makes possible His present engagement in defeating every power opposed to God (15:24). "For he must reign until he has put all his enemies under his feet" (15:25). The Corinthians' haughty and unrealistic sense of security (10:12) prevented them from taking the evil powers of this world seriously. How could they feel that they had won the victory over these powers when Christ was still defeating them? And "The last enemy to be destroyed is death" (15:26). They could hardly be living the life of the resurrection when victory over death was still outstanding.

The situation was similar to that of the heretics Paul spoke against in Philippians 3. They, too, thought that the perfection of resurrection life was already here. With respect to them, Paul said that he wanted to know Christ and the power of Christ's resurrection in the present, as well as the fellowship of Christ's suffering and death, so that he might attain the resurrection from the dead (3:10, 11). But it is one thing to know the power of the risen Christ in one's life now, and it is another to say we already have attained the resurrection. This is why Paul says:

"Not that I have obtained this or am already perfect" (3:12, RSV). What is certain now is that I belong to Jesus, but resurrection life is still ahead, and to that we must press on with energy, forgetting all else (3:13). So Paul says, "I press on toward the goal of the prize of the heavenly call of God in Christ Jesus" (3:14). Paul is still looking for the gold medal when the divine Judge calls him up to receive his prize (as in the Olympic games). It hasn't happened yet; so he just keeps racing on toward the goal line. The Philippian and Corinthian heretics needed this perspective of the future.

Practical arguments for the resurrection

Paul has been arguing that the resurrection of the dead is certain because of the resurrection of Christ. He turns now to two practical arguments for the resurrection, the first drawn from Corinthian baptismal practice and the second from his life as an apostle. The practices Paul refers to do not prove the resurrection, but they would not make sense if the resurrection were not true.

The first argument is known in logic as an ad hominum ("to the man") argument. Here you do not argue for the truth of something, but you take the beliefs or practices of others and use them against them. Paul refers to the Corinthian practice of baptism for the dead (1 Cor. 15:29). This is a variously interpreted text, but two major interpretations emerge. First, it is a proxy baptism whereby Christians were being baptized either for their pagan family members or friends, so as to assure meeting them in a future life, or for other believers who died before they were able to be baptized. Second, under the influence of their Christian relatives and friends, non-Christians may have been undergoing baptism as a possible guarantee of a future life with their Christian loved ones. No matter which view is espoused, Paul is saying this whole practice of baptism is without meaning if the resurrection is not true. If proxy baptism is being referred to, Paul was not condoning the practice, only showing how meaningless it would be without the resurrection.

Further, Paul says how absurd it would be for him to withstand danger every hour if the resurrection were not true! He testifies that he dies daily in that he daily puts his life on the line for Jesus. In its primary contextual meaning the verse is not referring to dying *to* one's sinful self but willingness to die *for* Christ, in the cause of the gospel. If there is no resurrection, why not "eat and drink for tomorrow we die" (15:32).

The nature of the resurrection body

With a spirit of unbelief certain Corinthians asked what kind of body resurrected people could have since the body had dissolved in the grave (15:35). To this supposedly wise question Paul presents two points. First, the death of the body, far from precluding life in a future body, actually sponsors it. Second, the body which is now, is not the body which shall be. To get these points across Paul uses two analogies. One is that of a seed planted in the ground. It does not come to life unless it dies, and God gives it a body which He has chosen (15:36, 37). The plant is in *continuity* with the seed, but is *different* from the seed. Ellen White states that while personal identity and character will be preserved in our resurrected bodies, the identical particles of matter will not. A much finer substance will compose those bodies (*Seventh-day Adventist Bible Commentary*, 6:1073).

Another analogy comes from the different kinds of bodies that exist in heaven and on earth. As Creator, God has created an appropriate body for everything. The inference is that He will create a body fit for resurrection life. This is a call to trust God as Creator. He who could call things into being from nothing at the creation of the world can certainly provide new bodies for his people.

The newness has to do with such elements as the following (15:44):

As Paul had earlier argued that the resurrected Christ was the

Present Body	**Future Body**
perishable	imperishable
dishonorable	glorious
weak	powerful
physical	spiritual

key to our resurrection, so now he argues that the risen Christ is the key to the nature of our new bodies—they will be like His! The first man, Adam, was from the earth (as Genesis 2 says), and the second man, Christ, is from heaven. The physical man comes first, then the spiritual—a counter to those Platonic views that made the original man spiritual, with the Fall accounting for the physical. No, first we bear the image of the man of dust, and then, at the end, we shall bear the image of the heavenly man. We will be like Jesus. That we will have a spiritual body does not mean the absence of a body, but a body which is the most appropriate vessel for the indwelling of the Holy Spirit.

So there is a big change coming. We, in our individuality and personhood, will be in the kingdom, but we will have new and glorious bodies like that of Christ. Our returning Lord "will transform the body of our humiliation that it may be conformed to the body of his glory, by the power that also enables him to make all things subject to himself" (Phil. 3:21). "Beloved, we are God's children now: what we will be has not yet been revealed. What we do know is this: when he is revealed we shall be like him" (1 John 3:2).

True, "flesh and blood" mankind as presently constituted (with the characteristics listed in 15:42-44, 50-54) cannot inherit God's kingdom (15:50). But God's new creation and transformation of His people in a twinkling of an eye will prepare us for the immortal world to come (15:51). Death will be defeated and its sting gone thanks to God, "who gives us the victory through our Lord Jesus Christ" (15:57).

The promise of what is to come is not a call to sit down and wait, but a challenge to be "steadfast, immovable, always excelling in the work of the Lord, because you know that in the Lord your labor is not in vain" (15:58). Our faith may be in vain if we deny the resurrection (15:14, 17), but if we affirm it with all our hearts, nothing we do will be in vain.

Heavenly Sabbaths

My first wife had had major surgery for cancer. On Sabbath morning, with her head now cleared from the anesthetic, she asked her Adventist nurse, "What day is it?" The nurse replied,

"It is the Sabbath." My wife responded, "Oh, Sabbaths will be nice in heaven." These were her last words just before she died. Now she and countless others, including ourselves the living, await the day of resurrection and transformation. "Our Lord, come!" (16:22).